Making the most of
CONIFERS
and *HEATHERS*

Adrian Bloom

floraprint

This edition published in the U.K. 1989 by
Burall Floraprint Ltd.,
Oldfield Lane, Wisbech, PE13 2TH.
Reprinted 1990, 1991, 1993, 1994

ISBN 0 903001 61 6

First published in the U.K. 1986 as
'Conifers and Heathers for a Year Round Garden'
for Aura Books and Floraprint Ltd. by
Marshall Cavendish Books Ltd. (ISBN 0 86307 489 8)

Printed in Singapore.

Adrian Bloom, the author of this book, is both a professional horticulturist and a keen gardener and plantsman. Through creating his now well-known garden at Bressingham from scratch, he fully appreciates the problems facing the modern gardener, whether the area is small or large. Not all home-owners can be expected to become enthusiastic gardeners, but this book shows what can be achieved to create a relatively trouble-free garden of year-round appeal.

Born in East Anglia, Adrian Bloom spent some early years in Canada, the United States and Europe before returning to his present home near Diss, Norfolk. He gained valuable experience abroad before joining the family business of Blooms Nurseries, begun by his father Alan Bloom, world-famous herbaceous specialist and creator of the Dell Garden at Bressingham. He now heads the company with his brother, Robert, having added conifers, heathers and shrubs to the specialist herbaceous perennial nursery founded by his father.

He is well known for his books, articles and television appearances, where he advocates a wider use and appreciation of plants, combining knowledge of good cultivation with the artistic use of plants in a variety of situations.

Contents

Introduction

The reasons for writing this book are many, but primarily I am attempting to illustrate, using one garden as the main example, what can be created by the average gardener to provide year round colour, form and foliage.

The keen and enthusiastic gardener will always be able to create a garden to fulfil his or her own needs and will be able to learn and adapt as it progresses. This book will, I hope, be of interest to them but I see it as giving guidance to the much larger band of people who have a garden, but are short of knowledge or ideas as to how to make the most of it.

There is little doubt as to the increase in popularity of dwarf conifers, heathers and dwarf shrubs as garden plants in recent years. What is, I think, so often a pity is that plants bought and planted in a garden are a disappointment to the owners because they have little or no idea as to how and where' they should be used to create the best effect. You have only to drive through some of our modern suburban housing estates to realize how little imagination is generally used and how limited is the range of plants. Not that any blame is attached to the home-owners: we can't all be expert gardeners, just as we can't all be expert mechanics or carpenters!

Although expert advice from books and garden centres is more available than it used to be, I can understand the frustrations that the new home-owner must feel in attempting to make an attractive garden to set off a new house. What plants to choose? How to design? What sort of garden to give pleasure the year round without too much work? The answer could lie in something similar to Mr and Mrs Edens' garden, illustrated and described in the following pages.

Let's get it straight, no garden is trouble free unless you put down concrete, but some types of gardens are a lot less work than others.

There are not really any short cuts to the first stage, whether you are starting from scratch or reorganizing an established garden: thorough preparation of the soil or planting areas is essential, and these early efforts will repay you in years to come.

This book takes you through that important early period of preparation and over a period of three years shows you how to go about creating your own year round garden. It is shown 'warts and all', with the problems that have occurred—they are the sort of problems that might arise in your garden—and suggests how you may overcome them. Mr and Mrs Edens had their losses, but as you can see in the photographs, they also had much to be proud of at the end of the three years—though the garden of course didn't stop at that point.

It is interesting, in this considerably revised and updated book, to see how the garden has matured in the ten years since it was first planted. With careful, but minimal maintenance it has developed into an individual garden with character and year round interest. It has also been extremely encouraging to me to discover how useful the original book has been to many would-be gardeners, many of whom have copied Mr and Mrs Edens' garden exactly.

This book, I hope, offers much more. It is a practical guide to how to make the most of dwarf conifers, heathers and dwarf shrubs, all of which lend themselves to the smaller garden, and most of which have year round appeal.

Why not take a fresh look at your garden and ask yourself if you are getting the most from it? For instance, what do you have to look at from November until March? In countries that are normally covered in snow during that period, perhaps there is no possibility of finding colour in the garden except for some deciduous shrubs and larger evergreens, but in Britain, Europe and many parts of the United States, winter is not so severe. Why not cheer yourself up in winter by using plants that give colour at that time of year in the garden? Is your lawn in front of the house achieving any purpose, except to give you the chore of cutting it each week through the summer? These and many other fundamental points should be questioned. This book will have achieved its object if it provides you with some of the answers.

The author's garden, *Juniperus squamata* 'Holger' is in the foreground.

Why conifers and heathers?

My interest in conifers and heathers began in 1963, soon after I returned from working abroad in the United States, Switzerland and Denmark to join my father Alan Bloom's nursery business. My father had established a well-known wholesale nursery and gardens at Bressingham in Norfolk, specializing in hardy perennials and alpines, had written many books and was already a recognized authority on these plants. It seemed to me that I would be forever in his shadow if I followed his footsteps exactly, much as I liked perennials and alpines, so I looked around for something to add to the business. No ideas are entirely original, and while visiting gardens in England I saw how attractive conifers and heathers could be in association with each other. My father was generous enough to give me, aged twenty-three, an area adjacent to his own five-acre Dell Garden. Truth to tell, I think he got fed up with me pestering him to let me plant conifers and heathers in his garden! My first plantings gave me the experience and knowledge to tackle my own garden when my wife and I moved into our new house in 1966.

From being somewhat uninterested in plants and with pretty scant knowledge I became, in my own words, 'extremely keen' and in my wife Rosemary's analysis 'fanatical'. Here, on rather a flat piece of ground on

heavy, rich loam, I had the opportunity to create my own garden. Unless you are a professional horticulturist (which I really wasn't, having had no formal horticultural education), I believe it is only when you reach the point of having your own home that you start seriously thinking about the garden.

Over a period of five years I dug, prepared and planted about half an acre round the house, sometimes digging by car headlights in the dark winter evenings. It was exciting, planning and watching the garden develop. I moved a lot of soil in trying to create undulations to make the design more interesting but also knew that in time the taller conifers in particular would enhance those humps, giving

shelter and structure to the garden.

As my interest grew, so did the garden and the range of plants. Although there were, of course, many people more expert than I on the subject of conifers, it seemed to me that no one was publicising them for use in the garden, particularly in association with heathers, and that some of the best conifers were just not known or available to the average gardener. This became somewhat of a crusade for me. I began to add a new line of plants to the perennials and alpines offered by the nursery.

The single most important point I soon learnt was that the 'dwarf' in 'dwarf conifers' could be misleading. Already, after five or six years, some conifers

Left This photograph of the author's garden was taken in September exactly twelve years after the house was built (see above). Previously an open meadow, this section was landscaped and planted within a period of five years.

described as dwarf in the books had grown well beyond that status. My garden was not only already full but some plants were certainly too close together. The time had come to expand and I managed—I'm not quite sure now how I did it—to persuade my brother Robert and my father to let me have the meadow in front of my house in which to develop the garden. This area comprised five acres, and was scheduled to be developed from 1973 over three or four years. It was quite an undertaking, but the results of mainly using conifers and heathers had provided a boost to the business and this was to be a display garden in which to try out new varieties and experiment with design and plant associations.

This expansion often prompted the comment from visitors that although they found the combination very attractive, conifers and heathers were obviously only suited to the larger garden. You can imagine that I did not take that lying down. I set out to prove that, contrary to this opinion, carefully selected dwarf conifers, heathers and dwarf shrubs are *ideally* suited to the smaller garden. Mr and Mrs Edens' garden and this book are very much the result of this belief.

The photographs, I think, say much more than words. Throughout the book they show gardens in winter and in summer. The undeniable advantage conifers and heathers have over many other plants is that they provide as much colour in winter

as in summer. The hundreds of interesting conifers now available from garden centres or specialist nurseries give an incredible range of colour, form and foliage, many of which change through the seasons. Even now this fact is seldom recognised by the average gardener or home-owner, the very person who is likely to benefit most from using these plants because of their low maintenance.

There are probably over a thousand or more varieties of heathers, although a hundred would more than cover the range for all but the collector or enthusiast. These too can create a patchwork of changing colours; it is possible to find forms which will provide flowers for eleven months of the year, but those with coloured foliage give an equal variation the year round. It has to be said that heathers can have their drawbacks. Nearly all the summer flowering varieties will not tolerate lime in the soil, but there are ways round that one (see page 76); many heathers will not take extreme low temperatures without snow cover, nor will they generally

5

Photographed in March, the author's garden gives a wonderful display.

tolerate hot, dry or arid conditions—but that is not likely to be too great a problem to British gardeners.

Alternatives to heathers

If you cannot grow heathers (erica and calluna) successfully, to provide you with year round colour, there are alternatives according to your location. Dwarf shrubs are an obvious range of plants to mix with conifers, particularly in the smaller garden. Evergreens such as *Euonymus fortunei* and its varieties with golden and variegated foliage, or deciduous shrubs such as the dwarf Berberis with coloured leaves for example. Dwarf perennials and alpines associate well, as do the dwarfer spring bulbs.

From time to time of course, all gardeners have losses due to one cause or another. When you get interested in plants it is always a temptation to try those which are perhaps not quite reliably winter hardy in your own particular climate. I have plants in my garden that have come from all over the world and it is a challenge to see how they will perform, but inevitably there are successes and failures. If the plants do succeed, we can safely produce them for sale and recommend them to British gardeners. New plants are always of interest. In the United States of America hardiness zones are given as a guide to nurseries and private gardeners alike, and plants are categorized according to the minimum temperature they will tolerate to succeed. This is only a guide since many individual gardens will be able to grow successfully plants not considered hardy enough by the experts. For instance, a shaded or sheltered location is likely to be much more favourable to many plants than an exposed one. Spring frosts can be a nightmare in many gardens, including my own, but, as I have mentioned, no garden is perfect.

Satisfaction is not guaranteed in gardening but—like many other things in life—you get out what you put in. I have had and continue to have a tremendous amount of satisfaction from my own garden, and as time goes on it becomes even more of a challenge to alter and adapt it as it matures. I am reluctantly having to part with some conifers that are perhaps too big or planted too closely or are too similar to other types. However, when such a conifer is removed it leaves a space which can be filled by other interesting plants—and there is never any shortage of them. The trees I planted several years ago are now providing shade and shelter for bulbs, shade-loving perennials and shrubs. Old groups of heathers here and there can be removed to make way for raised peat beds on which can be planted a range of acid-loving shrubs, alpines and perennials. My only regret is that pressure of business and other commitments prevent me from having more time to spend in the garden.

I was once accused by an eminent horticulturist of promoting an idea 'that was not gardening'. Any gardener worth his salt, the argument continued, would always want to be adding new plants to his garden, to be changing and developing and would not and *should* not be tied down to such a narrow range of plants. He was missing the point. The last thing I would wish to do is to advocate that everyone puts their garden down to conifers and heathers, although I believe every garden would be poorer without some of these plants. The keen gardeners can look after themselves—but they represent only 10 per cent or less of those people with gardens. What I am trying to do is to reach the other 90 per cent with some ideas which will give them the opportunity to create a garden of lasting pleasure. I rest my case, only adding that I hope you enjoy the book.

6

The Edens' garden

In order to show how conifers and heathers could be used in a small garden I first had to find a garden. The *Eastern Daily Press* and its local paper were only too happy to inform their readers that I was looking for a garden and that our company, Blooms Nurseries, would provide plants free of charge.

From the tremendous response (within a 10-mile radius of Bressingham) I shortlisted five gardens and went to see them and their owners.

Mr and Mrs Edens had the perfect site; a 20 × 10m (60 × 30ft) front garden on an eight to ten year old housing development in Diss. The soil was a mixture of clay and sandy loam which they had imported. The garden as shown had two narrow borders planted with none too healthy roses and a wider border near the road which had a selection of shrubs and one pampas grass.

They were amenable to having the old plants cleared out and starting afresh, which was essential to my ideas.

This was the first week of September 1975 and the ground was rock hard and plants had to be dug out with pickaxes!

Within two weeks with the stalwart help of three of our nurserymen the garden was cleared, prepared, planned and planted.

The *South Norfolk News* faithfully recorded the change.

Planning the garden

Whatever your garden size or location, it is worth taking time to think about what sort of garden you would like. If you are moving into an older house with an established garden your options may, of course, be limited, although, even here, it is worth approaching the garden with a fresh eye: after all, most people bring or buy their own furniture for a new house, or make internal alterations such as redecorating —so why not do the same outside? Perhaps there is an old tree, conifer, hedge or shrub that would be better for being removed.

Is your garden on the flat, a slope or a hill? Each location has its advantages and disadvantages. If your garden is flat, why not try to make a few undulations, firstly with the soil, secondly by using plants to enhance this sense of scale. If you are on a slope you have an ideal opportunity to use it to your advantage by planning the beds and borders to give a natural surround to the incline. A path or stream could provide the central line.

Even if you are on a hill don't despair. Conifers, heathers,

New garden of Edens

Mrs. Angela Edens and her children Denise, Teresa and Gina in their garden at 27, Walcot Rise, Diss before staff from Blooms Nurseries of Bressingham gave it a new look.

Mr. Adrian Bloom is pictured above putting the finishing touches to the garden which has been transformed with informal curving beds, dwarf and slow-growing conifers of various shades of green and colourful heathers. The project is designed to show in a small garden the advantage of minimum-upkeep plants.

Press interest from the *South Norfolk News*.

shrubs and alpines can be planted on terraces.

Mr and Mrs Edens' plot was flat, but by making some slight undulations which were not out of keeping with neighbouring gardens we were able to change the garden from a formal to an informal one. The idea was to create a restful scene which would provide colour year round. A draft sketch on paper was all that was required, the detailed plan being drawn up afterwards.

How to plant from a plan

Assuming you have all the correct measurements, mark out beds and borders on the same scale as that given on your plan. (More details follow on page 10.) As a general precaution take your time in measuring if you are copying directly from a plan: if you are anything like me at mathematics, mistakes can easily be made at this stage, leading to untold problems later. If you have gone wrong, it should not be too disastrous as long as you remember to space out *all* plants indicated for a particular bed prior to starting to plant. This way you can adjust the plants yourself so that the bed is not overcrowded at one end and left standing without plants at the other.

The Edens' garden photographed in the spring following planting.

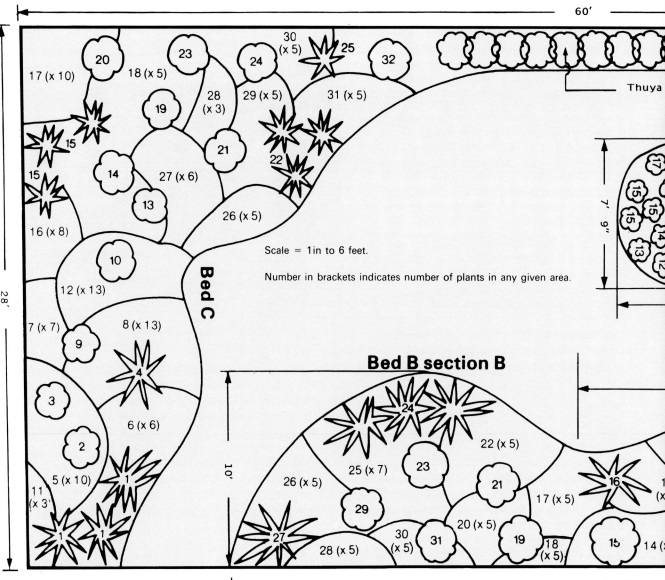

60'

17 (x 10)   20   18 (x 5)   23   24   30 (x 5)   25   32   Thuya

28 (x 3)   29 (x 5)   31 (x 5)

19   21   15   15   14   27 (x 6)   22   13   16 (x 8)   26 (x 5)

17   15   15   14   13   12   7' 9"

10   12 (x 13)   Bed C

7 (x 7)   8 (x 13)   9   4   3   6 (x 6)   2   5 (x 10)   1   11 (x 3')   1   1

Scale = 1in to 6 feet.

Number in brackets indicates number of plants in any given area.

28'

10'

Bed B section B

24   22 (x 5)   25 (x 7)   23   21   26 (x 5)   29   16   1 (x   17 (x 5)   27   30 (x 5)   31   20 (x 5)   19   18 (x 5)   15   14 (x   28 (x 5)

41' 6"

Planting plan

Bed A

1 *Abies balsamea* 'Hudsonia'
2 *Juniperus squamata* 'Pygmaea'
3 *Thuya plicata* 'Rogersii'
4 *Chamaecyparis lawsoniana* 'Pygmaea Argentea'
5 *Picea mariana* 'Nana'
6 *Chamaecyparis pisifera* 'Nana Aurea Variegata'
7 *Chamaecyparis obtusa* 'Nana'
8 *Picea abies* 'Little Gem'
9 *Juniperus squamata* 'Blue Star'
10 *Thuya occidentalis* 'Danica'
11 *Chamaecyparis pisifera* 'Nana'
12 *Chamaecyparis obtusa* 'Nana Lutea'
13 *Cryptomeria japonica* 'Vilmoriniana'
14 *Juniperus communis* 'Compressa'
15 *Chamaecyparis lawsoniana* 'Minima Aurea'
16 *Chamaecyparis obtusa* 'Kosteri'
17 *Chamaecyparis lawsoniana* 'Gnome'
18 *Thuya orientalis* 'Aurea Nana'
19 *Chamaecyparis lawsoniana* 'Minima Glauca'

Bed B section A

1 *Juniperus communis* 'Repanda'
2 *Erica carnea* 'Pink Spangles'
3 *Arabis ferdinand-coburgii* 'Variegata'
4 *Thuya occidentalis* 'Rheingold'
5 *Erica cinerea* 'C. D. Eason'
6 *Juniperus horizontalis* 'Hughes'
7 *Erica x darleyensis* 'Darley Dale'
8 *Picea glauca* 'Albertiana Conica'
9 *Calluna vulgaris* 'Robert Chapman'
10 *Calluna vulgaris* 'Silver Queen'
11 *Calluna vulgaris* 'Darkness'
12 *Chamaecyparis lawsoniana* 'Ellwood's Gold'
13 *Dianthus* 'Prichard's Variety'
14 *Ajuga reptans* 'Purpurea'
15 *Chamaecyparis pisifera* 'Boulevard'
16 *Juniperus squamata* 'Holger'

Bed B section B

17 *Erica erigena* 'W. T. Rackliff'
18 *Acaena buchananii*
19 *Chamaecyparis pisifera* 'Plumosa Aurea Nana'
20 *Euonymus radicans* 'Emerald Gaiety'
21 *Chamaecyparis pisifera* 'Filifera Nana'
22 *Erica carnea* 'King George'
23 *Thuya orientalis* 'Aurea Nana'
24 *Juniperus horizontalis* 'Glauca'
25 *Erica cinerea* 'Pink Ice'
26 *Calluna vulgaris* 'Golden Carpet'
27 *Calluna taxifolia* var. *lutchuensis* (syn. *maritima*)
28 *Sempervivum* 'Othello'
29 *Juniperus chinensis* 'Pyramidalis'
30 *Phlox subulata* 'Temiscaming'
31 *Thuya occidentalis* 'Holmstrup'

Bed C

1 *Juniperus sabina* 'Tamariscifolia'
2 *Thuya orientalis* 'Conspicua'
3 *Thuya occidentalis* 'Smaragd'
4 *Taxus baccata* 'Repens Aurea'
5 *Hebe pinguifolia* 'Pagei'
6 *Erica vagans* 'Mrs. Maxwell'
7 *Hedera helix* 'Chicago'
8 *Erica carnea* 'Myretoun Ruby'
9 *Chamaecyparis lawsoniana* 'Nana Albospica'
10 *Chamaecyparis lawsoniana* 'Blue Nantais'
11 *Hedera helix* 'Silver Queen'
12 *Erica carnea* 'Foxhollow'
13 *Chamaecyparis obtusa* 'Nana Gracilis'
14 *Thuya occidentalis* 'Lutescens'
15 *Juniperus horizontalis* 'Plumosa Compacta'
16 *Euonymus fortunei* 'Variegatus'
17 *Euonymus fortunei* 'Emerald 'n' Gold'
18 *Berberis thunbergii* 'Atropurpurea Nana'
19 *Juniperus scopulorum* 'Springbank'
20 *Chamaecyparis lawsoniana* 'Ellwoodii'
21 *Chamaecyparis pisifera* 'Filifera Aurea'
22 *Juniperus squamata* 'Blue Carpet'
23 *Thuya occidentalis* 'Lutea Nana'
24 *Cryptomeria japonica* 'Lobbii Nana'
25 *Taxus baccata* 'Semperaurea'
26 *Erica carnea* 'Springwood White'
27 *Erica x darleyensis* 'Furzey' (syn. 'Cherry Stevens')
28 *Calluna vulgaris* 'H. E. Beale'
29 *Erica vagans* 'Lyonesse'
30 *Erica x darleyensis* 'Arthur Johnson'
31 *Erica carnea* 'Vivellii'
32 *Picea pungens* 'Globosa'

Bed D

1 *Taxus baccata* 'Standishii'
2 *Taxus baccata* 'Repandens'
3 *Juniperus sabina* 'Blue Danube'
4 *Juniperus x media* 'Old Gold'
5 *Tsuga canadensis* 'Jeddeloh'
6 *Chamaecyparis pisifera* 'Squarrosa Sulphurea'
7 *Juniperus scopulorum* 'Blue Heaven'
8 *Chamaecyparis lawsoniana* 'Tamariscifolia'
9 *Juniperus virginiana* 'Grey Owl'
10 *Taxus baccata* 'Summergold'
11 *Erica cinerea* 'Purple Beauty'
12 *Erica x darleyensis* 'Silberschmelze'
13 *Erica x darleyensis* 'J. H. Brummage'
14 *Hedera helix* 'Silver Queen'
15 *Erica carnea* 'Myretoun Ruby'
16 *Thuya occidentalis* 'Smaragd'
17 *Thuya plicata* 'Stoneham Gold'
18 *Juniperus scopulorum* 'Skyrocket'
19 *Juniperus procumbens* 'Nana'
20 *Juniperus x media* 'Sulphur Spray'
21 *Erica carnea* 'Springwood Pink'
22 *Ajuga reptans* 'Burgundy Glow'

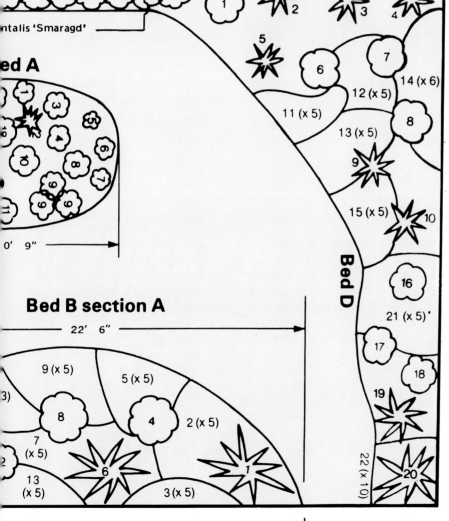

Making a start

Although in the next few pages I shall be describing in detail what we did in Mr and Mrs Edens' garden, the advice holds good for anyone starting a garden, or remaking a garden or part of one.

There are places for formal gardens but to my mind most suburban gardens are not one of them, particularly if you plan to use conifers, heathers and a range of other hardy ornamental garden plants. Therefore we decided to dig up the formal rows of roses, many of which were not growing well, and to start afresh.

Whether the garden is new or established thorough preparation is essential. If you have a new garden site it is quite likely that it will not only have builder's rubble and lumps of clay and subsoil near the surface but may well have perennial weeds lurking under it. What to do? Well, firstly, don't rush into planting or even consider it until you have had time to assess what you have in the way of soil conditions. Subsoil or heavy clay can be improved and broken down if there is not too much of it, but it may be worth getting rid of it and importing some good top-soil. Depending on the time of year you take over the garden you must decide whether and how soon you can treat any perennial weeds. There are weedkillers which if used according to the manufacturers' instructions can kill perennial thistle, couch grass and other invasive weeds though mostly these will have to be treated whilst in growth. Though you may not be so unlucky to have these or other perennial weeds greet you when you move

The line of the beds is marked out with stakes knocked into the ground.

A spit of soil is taken out and the bottom of the trench forked over.

into the garden do remember that digging and eradication of them should precede the marking out of borders.

Planning and marking out borders

The method I advocate, whether you are making your own design or following someone else's, is to knock in sticks or stakes either to get a visual idea of how the borders will look or to known measurements if you are following a plan. You can then alter them according to your wishes, prior to final marking out. String, rope or a hosepipe can be stretched round the inside of the stakes to create curves which can then be followed when you are cutting out the shapes with a spade.

Having cut the outline of the bed, the turf is then removed.

Soil preparation

If the soil is heavy, medium or light, thorough digging to a depth of between 35-45cm (14-18in) or so will help to allow aeration, drainage and weathering before planting. If your soil is heavy the bottom of the trench may need breaking up with a fork to allow extra drainage and possibly some sharp grit or sand mixed with it. It will certainly help to dig before winter, allowing the frost and wind to break down the soil and plant when drier in the Spring. If you have or can obtain a weed-free compost or, better still, peat it will definitely improve the soil if you incorporate it whilst digging. All this may sound like hard work but there is no escaping it. Of course, if your garden is on light weed-free soil, rather than on heavy clay, with builder's rubble and perennial weeds, this work will not be so difficult.

Soil testing

The pH or acid or alkaline levels of your soil will determine to some extent what plants you can expect to grow successfully, so it is quite important to test the soil. Full details on soil testing are given on page 75, together with ideas on how you can adapt your soil to grow summer-flowering heathers, rhododendrons and other acid-loving plants.

Finding the plants

Where should you start looking? Most reputable garden centres stock heathers and a range of conifers, but it is worth searching out the specialist nurseryman or garden centre who will have available a good range of both.

Choose the varieties carefully: those selected for Mr and Mrs Edens' garden are distinct and reliable. Some other suggestions will be shown and described later.

Planting time

Almost any time is suitable for planting as long as the soil is in good condition and you use plants that have been grown in pots or containers. Autumn and spring remain the most favourable months for planting although summer planting can continue as long as plants are watered thoroughly at the time of planting and throughout dry periods.

It may not always be possible to plant immediately. In spring, summer or autumn keep plants from drying out, and if necessary in winter protect them from heavy frosts until it is possible to plant.

Planting conifers

Most of the advice that can be given for planting conifers would be equally applicable to other woody plants—and for that matter, for most plants grown in containers. Few open ground or rootballed conifers are offered these days by nurserymen or garden centres although most are quite satisfactorily handled from early autumn to late spring if purchased this way. The section on moving a large conifer (see page 38) covers this advice quite adequately.

It is important to buy your conifers from a reputable nursery, garden centre or specialist grower. I have seen conifers in some garden centres that were fit only for the rubbish heap—plants starved, lacking in colour, very woody and bare at the base—all

If dry, soak the plants before planting. Peat-based compost dries out quickly.

Set out the plants in their containers before starting to plant.

Using a spade, prepare a hole. Knock the plant from its pot.

Set the plant in the hole. Pull some soil round the rootball and firm.

the things one should try to avoid. Sometimes, if a plant has been in a pot too long, it will also have a very congested root system with the larger roots circling the base of the pot. Such a plant is unlikely to establish satisfactorily. Conifers should look healthy, whatever their natural colour, and with the exception of some of the pines, be well furnished at the base. The foliage should be down to ground level or to the top of the pot rim, with no brown or bare patches. The plant should have roots to the sides of the pot but not be overly potbound and it should be labelled. By this I mean that it should have a full botanical name with some description as to habit and probable rate of growth in 10 years.

Back to planting. When your plants are to hand and the soil is thoroughly prepared, the next steps are relatively simple. The rule is the same for both small and large plants: dig the hole, making sure the soil is friable (if it is not the addition of peat will be essential), and after carefully removing the pot, insert the conifer at the correct depth. This is generally determined by the level of the soil at the top of the container which should be level or just below the finished soil level. The advice given below should be followed for all container grown plants. A detailed list of the dwarf varieties used in this bed is given on page 15 and many others are described in detail in other sections in the book.

Planting heathers

Included under the name heathers are the summer flowering and foliage forms of the lings, *Calluna vulgaris* and the heaths, botanically appearing under the name *Erica*. The heaths include both summer and winter flowering species and numerous cultivars or varieties.

All are evergreen shrubs, and vary from miniature forms growing less than 10cm (5in) in height to the tree heaths that reach as much as 2-3m (6-9ft).

Flowers and foliage

Some heathers, such as *Erica carnea* 'Foxhollow', seldom flower but give a marvellous display of coloured foliage the year round. But heathers are really valuable as garden plants because among them are varieties which when selected carefully can provide practically twelve months of continuous flower. No other group of plants can boast of such advantages. Also those usually dull winter months in the garden can be brightened by winter flowering ericas. *Erica darleyensis* 'Arthur Johnson', for instance, flowers most years from late November until early May—good garden value indeed!

The hardiness factor

In my introduction I have indicated that most heathers—or, to be exact, heaths and heathers—are hardy throughout the British Isles with the exception of some species from South Africa and the Southern Hemisphere which are used as house plants or for bedding. Some of the summer flowering heathers such as *Erica cinerea*, the bell heather and *Erica vagans*, the Cornish heath, can be damaged in severe winters, but by and large British gardeners can consider themselves perfectly situated to make the most of these plants.

After thorough preparation dig a hole where required. Leave room for the addition of moist peat.

After soaking the peat put a spadeful or a double handful in the planting hole. Mix lightly with soil.

Position the plant in the prepared hole, setting it with the top of the rootball level with the soil.

This is not the case for many would-be heather gardeners in the United States and Canada. A select range seems reasonably successful in the north-western states and Vancouver area—a climate not unlike Britain's. In other northern and eastern areas *Erica carnea*, the winter flowering heather, and its varieties are hardy as are most callunas—with snow cover or some protection from drying winds. But in these areas the problem can be extreme and the prolonged summer heat is intolerable to many heathers. See my notes earlier in the book on page 6 and the section which deals with alternatives to heathers on page 48.

Likes and dislikes

Like most plants heathers have their likes and dislikes—and some of the dislikes are quite fundamental. Summer flowering ericas and all callunas will not tolerate lime. This does mean that at a garden such as that planted at Mr and Mrs Edens', summer flowering varieties would need to be substituted on soils containing lime. A list of plants for limy or alkaline soils is suggested in the bed plant lists. It *is* possible to grow summer flowering forms successfully if large amounts of peat are used and regular watering is carried out with a chemical containing an iron chelate.

A little-known but proven method of changing your soil from a high pH (alkaline or limy) to a lower pH (acid) is to use a chemical called flowers of sulphur. Details of this seemingly revolutionary method and how to use it are given on page 76, together with the method by which you can test the pH of your soil.

Heathers do not like extremes of moisture or drought. Good drainage is required for successful growing and this is where the

12

Pull soil and peat around the plant, ensuring that the peat does not bury the foliage.

Firm the soil around the plant with the foot and level surrounding soil.

Fork around the plant where the soil has become compressed to allow aeration and drainage.

For best results, work a mulch of peat or composted bark around the plants to a depth of 3–5cm (1½–2in).

importance of preparation comes in. Mix plenty of peat with very heavy soils to provide aeration. On sandy or very well drained soils peat acts to retain moisture but should not be allowed to dry out too much.

Heathers with golden foliage generally require full sun and although some plants are tolerant of shade they will not succeed or flower well where shade is too dense or conditions too dry.

Like most plants, heathers just need to be given a fair chance. It is also useful to know that most heathers and many other shrubs and conifers are grown in the nursery in a compost containing no soil. It is therefore helpful to assist quick establishment of that plant if peat can be mixed in with the soil when planting. Plant singly or in groups at distances of about 30-45cm (12-18in), according to variety.

Mulching

Heathers tend to make new roots near the surface. A mulch or covering of peat or composted bark will assist this rooting though it is not essential. However, mulching also helps to protect roots in winter, retain moisture in summer and keep down annual weeds—all beneficial.

The illustrations show you clearly how to plant heathers and get them off to a good start.

The garden planted

The garden from start to finish took about two weeks to complete. The total number of man-hours could be estimated at about eighty to one hundred. Conditions were far from ideal, in fact the ground was so hard that during preparation for planting a pickaxe was required for breaking up the subsoil!

This preparation is absolutely necessary to give plants a good start but conditions in late autumn or winter would be more favourable for working the soil. I and my helpers were trying to create an instant garden! Householders are generally impatient to get plants into the ground but it is far better to take time in preparation to avoid problems later.

Cost

When you furnish your house it costs money. When you furnish the garden it will also cost money. But there are both expensive ways and cheap ways of gaining the same objective with the difference between the two primarily a matter of time. Later in the book are shown the stages that are gone through to produce plants and particularly conifers. Obviously you can buy smaller three- to four-year-old plants much more cheaply than those that are 10 years old—but you will then have to wait longer for the smaller plants to grow. Most of the conifers used in planting Mr and Mrs Edens' garden were two to five years old and the heathers one to two years.

Additional costs were in peat and, again, this can be adjusted according to your pocket and whatever else you may be able to use as a cheaper substitute —remembering that whatever you choose it should be well rotted or composted and not contain weed seeds.

Who can say what is expensive? It will cost you money to lay out a new garden from scratch but it needn't be done all at once. It is my contention (and I'm sticking to it!) that a good garden is an investment and will quite often increase the value of your property when you wish to resell. It will also give you a lot of interest, pleasure and satisfaction in its creation.

Easy stages

If the cost of attempting to create an 'instant garden' such as we planted at Mr and Mrs Edens' is too prohibitive or if the size 20 × 10m (60 × 30ft) is too large then why not plan in easy stages? Take one bed or border as shown on the plan and in the final photographs at a time—or that which suits your area. You could create a complete garden similar to the Edens' in three years instead of a few weeks or months and spread the effort and cost.

Personal choice

I have made a suggested planting

Dwarf conifer bed immediately after planting. The mulch surrounding the plant is of sedge peat.

plan based on my experience and my selection of varieties. It is a question of personal choice whether you stick to this plan or substitute other varieties. Although most of the conifers, heathers and shrubs are likely to be available on the majority of garden centres in the UK it may be that if something is unobtainable a suitable substitute will need to be made anyway. Some plants on the plan opposite are only suitable for acid or lime free soils. Alternative suggestions for alkaline soils are made within individual plant lists.

The Conifer Bed A

This bed which we planted in Mr and Mrs Edens' garden would be suitable for any small garden. All plants are in the category of 'dwarf'. Perhaps this would be an appropriate point to mention what I mean by the terms dwarf, slow growing, medium and large when applied to growth rates of conifers.

Large

Those conifers which grow to 3m (9ft) or over in ten years and ultimately over 12m (36ft).

Medium

Applies to those types that grow between 1.5-3m (5-9ft) in ten years, ultimately reaching 8-12m (24-36ft)—although some may grow to more than 12m (36ft).

Slow growing

This term encompasses some of the medium growers, but basically means those growing to 1.5-2.5m (5-8ft) in ten years and ultimately 6-10m (18-30ft).

Dwarf

These would be conifers which grow less than 1.5m (5ft) in ten years. Because of the tremendous variety in this range—some forms may never reach 1.5m (5ft) even after fifty years—it is impossible to generalise in estimating eventual height.

There are also prostrate i.e. flat growing and semi-prostrate i.e. spreading conifers to which separate dimensions apply, giving both height and spread. All the descriptive lists of conifers on pages 54-69 give ten year estimates only.

I should point out that these figures are and can be only approximate since different soil conditions, rainfall, climate and aspect all affect rates of growth.

Below are comments made on the particular varieties used in the Edens' garden and some suggested alternatives where supplies may be limited or unobtainable.

List of dwarf conifers, island bed A

1. *Abies balsamea* 'Hudsonia'. Dwarf form of the 'Balsam fir'. Dark green leaves, bright green shoots in spring.

*2. *Juniperus squamata* 'Pygmaea'. Grey-green foliage, nodding branch tips. Alternative *Juniperus recurva* 'Embley Park', dark green foliage, similar habit. May need slight trimming.

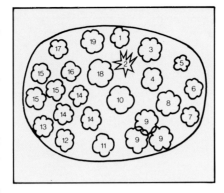

*3. *Thuja plicata* 'Rogersii'. Coppery golden foliage, good winter colour, rounded habit.

*4. *Chamaecyparis lawsoniana* 'Pygmaea Argentea'. A beautiful form, blue-green foliage, tipped white.

5. *Picea mariana* 'Nana'. Very slow, compact, bun-shaped spruce. Blue-grey foliage. Alternative *Picea glauca* 'Echiniformis' is very similar, slightly more open and vigorous.

6. *Chamaecyparis pisifera* 'Nana Aurea Variegata'. Flattish, bun-shaped miniature with green foliage flecked white and yellow.

7. *Chamaecyparis obtusa* 'Nana'. Another miniature with glossy green foliage, compact, rounded habit. Alternative *Chamaecyparis lawsoniana* 'Green Globe', rounded, moss-like ball of green foliage.

8. *Picea abies* 'Little Gem'. Dense, rounded ball of green, attractive when new shoots appear in spring. Attractive to red spider mite also (see page 44). Alternative *P. glauca* 'Alberta Globe' also liked by red spider mites.

*9. *Juniperus squamata* 'Blue Star'. Deservedly one of the most popular dwarf conifers. Steel-blue foliage, nodding tips, very adaptable.

*10. *Thuja occidentalis* 'Danica'. Deep green foliage held in vertical layers. Slightly bronze in winter. Alternative possibly *Thuja occidentalis* 'Hertz Midget',

rounded green bush.

11. *Chamaecyparis pisifera* 'Nana'. Slow-growing, bun-shaped, green.

12. *Chamaecyparis obtusa* 'Nana Lutea'. A very choice form with bright golden yellow foliage the year round.

13. *Cryptomeria japonica* 'Vilmoriniana'. Tightly compressed habit, green in summer, bronze-green in winter. Alternative *Chamaecyparis lawsoniana*, 'Pygmy', dwarf green.

14. *Juniperus communis* 'Compressa'. 'The Noah's Ark Juniper', a real miniature, columnar and very compact.

15. *Chamaecyparis lawsoniana* 'Minima Aurea'. One of the best. Slow-growing, clear yellow foliage winter and summer, compact, pyramidal habit.

*16. *Chamaecyparis obtusa* 'Kosteri'. Rather scarce, upright form, flattened, twisted sprays of bright green. Alternative perhaps a completely different colour, *Picea pungens* 'Globosa', dwarf blue spruce.

17. *Chamaecyparis lawsoniana* 'Gnome'. Compact, rounded bush with congested dark green leaves. Alternative *Chamaecyparis lawsoniana* 'Green Globe', similar but even more compact.

*18. *Thuja orientalis* 'Aurea Nana'. Always attractive with bright golden yellow 'laminated' foliage sprays in summer, bronzing in winter.

*19. *Chamaecyparis lawsoniana* 'Minima Glauca'. Globular bush of sea-green. Alternative *Chamaecyparis lawsoniana* 'Gimbornii', similar, but with softer, denser foliage sprays.

The above comprises a good selection although some are much slower growing than others. Those marked with an asterisk required a little more space left around them when planting.

Bed B

If you follow a plan from a magazine or a book without allowing for your own soil or site, it can lead to less than successful results. Study carefully to see if advice is given in order that you can adapt plans or varieties to suit your situation.

Since, in my own garden, I seldom put pencil to paper, preferring to plan from viewing and memory, the planning of the Edens' garden was an interesting exercise. Of course, one has to plan in order to know what is needed to achieve the required results.

Plants must be bought and fitted together to form a cohesive pattern. Nevertheless, do not be afraid to adapt a plan to fit a quite different site or bed shape. You can get an idea of what plants should fit together from the plants in the Edens' garden. Of course, this was planned as a whole and for anyone with a similar site—of approximately 20 × 10m (60 × 30ft)—the complete plan can be followed.

Plans for small areas

On the other hand, the plans for the Edens' garden can conveniently be divided into sections which could easily be fitted into a smaller area. Take your pick. On this page and the next few pages you can find the following information:
a) Detailed plans.
b) Photographs taken of each planted plan immediately after planting and three years later.
c) Lists of each plant used, their advantages and disadvantages noted.
d) Brief cultural notes and suggested alternatives for alkaline soils are given. Suggested alternatives are also given where the plant or plants may be difficult to obtain.

NOTE—Reference to future work to be undertaken applies from a three year after planting

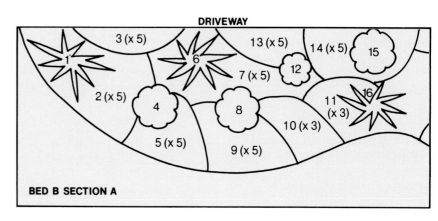

DRIVEWAY

BED B SECTION A

period—i.e. plants four to five years old. Comments made apply specifically to the plans and results obtained in the Edens' garden but can mostly be generally applied.

All plants are lime tolerant unless stated otherwise.

List of plants used in bed B section A

1. *Juniperus communis* 'Repanda'. Excellent ground cover conifer. Will need some pruning each year to prevent too wide a spread.

2. *Erica carnea* 'Pink Spangles'. Low spreading winter flowering heather. May be necessary to trim away from base of *Thuja* 'Rheingold'. Do this in late April.

3. *Arabis ferdinand-coburgii* 'Variegata'. Prostrate, dwarf, prettily variegated alpine. Tendency to revert to green—these shoots should be cut away. Alternative *Phlox amoena* 'Variegata'.

4. *Thuja occidentalis* 'Rheingold'. A popular dwarf conifer changing colour with the seasons. Initially very slow growing it can, after some years, become quite large. Although the natural shape is broadly pyramidal it can become rather open and wide spreading. Suggest when plant reaches 40-50cm (16-20in) trimming it at least every other year.

5. *Erica cinerea* 'C. D. Eason'. Summer flowering heather, dark green foliage, red flowers. Trim

old flower heads back each March or April. Dislikes lime. Alternative for alkaline soils a) *Erica carnea* 'Ruby Glow'—winter flowering heather, or b) *Berberis thunbergii* 'Baggatelle', purple-foliaged, dwarf shrub.

6. *Juniperus horizontalis* 'Hughes'. Bright silver-blue, prostrate conifer. Will need annual trim to prevent too wide a spread. Alternative *J. horizontalis* 'Blue Chip'.

7. *Erica darleyensis* 'Darley Dale'. Pink, long-flowering winter heather. Outer edges will need annual trim to prevent them growing into conifers. Alternative *E. carnea* 'Myretoun Ruby'.

8. *Picea glauca* 'Albertiana Conica'. A real favourite miniature forest tree—also favourite with insects! Spray in spring (twice within two weeks) with systemic insecticide and repeat in summer during periods of hot dry weather. Evening is best to avoid scorching foliage. Alternative *P. omorika* 'Nana', the dwarf Serbian spruce.

9. *Calluna vulgaris* 'Robert Chapman'. Golden foliaged ling. Trim back each spring. Dislikes lime. Alternative for alkaline soils *Erica carnea* 'Aurea', winter flowering heather with golden foliage.

10. *Calluna vulgaris* 'Silver Queen'. Silver-grey foliaged, summer flowering heather. Trim back hard each spring. Alternative for alkaline soils: a) *Erica carnea* 'Springwood White', winter

Bed B, section A photographed immediately after planting.

The same section of bed photographed three years later.

Dislikes alkaline soils. Alternatives: a) *Erica carnea* 'Vivellii', winter flowering heather, bronze foliage, carmine flowers, or b) *Sedum spurium* 'Purple Carpet', an alpine with red foliage and rosy red flowers in summer (seven plants would be required to fill space).

12. *Chamaecyparis lawsoniana* 'Ellwood's Gold'. Popular, upright conifer, gold-tinged foliage.

13. *Dianthus* 'Prichard's Variety', a silver-foliaged alpine with pink flowers in summer. Spreading habit but not invasive. Keep trimmed away from base of conifer. Alternative variety *Dianthus* 'Garland'.

14. *Ajuga reptans* 'Purpurea'. Purple-leaved, ground covering alpine. Spreads quickly but may die out in patches after winter, also blue flowers in spring will seed. Pull out inferior seedlings, replant bare patches in April. Prevent from growing into conifers or other plants. Alternative *Ajuga reptans* 'Burgundy Glow'.

15. *Chamaecyparis pisifera* 'Boulevard'. Blue, pyramidal-shaped, slow growing conifer. Dislikes shallow, chalky soils, dry or too wet conditions. Use ample peat when planting, keep watered if dry in summer. Trimming from when the plant is 40-50cm (16-20in) high will help keep foliage dense. Alternative for highly alkaline soils: a) *Juniperus chinensis* 'Robusta Green', upright, irregular habit, or b) *Taxus baccata* 'Fastigiata Robusta', narrow, upright, deep rich green foliage.

16. *Juniperus squamata* 'Holger'. Prostrate conifer creamy white foliage in spring and summer. Will need pruning occasionally to avoid spreading too wide. Needs sunny position.

flowering heather, or b) *Potentilla mandschurica,* dwarf white, summer flowering, silver foliaged shrubs, or c) *Hebe pinguifolia* 'Pagei', silver-blue, hardy dwarf shrub with white flower spikes.

11. *Calluna vulgaris* 'Darkness'. Summer flowering heather, requires trimming each spring.

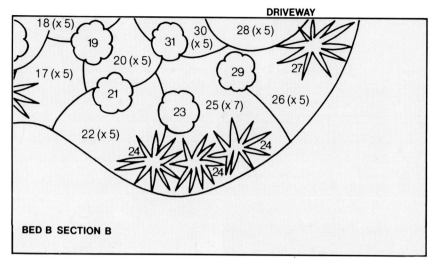

BED B SECTION B

Bed B, section B after planting.

Bed B section B

17. *Erica erigena* 'W. T. Rackliff'. A late spring flowering heather of neat habit, white flowers. Alternative *E. carnea* 'Springwood White'.

18. *Acaena buchananii*. This is a spreading, mat-forming alpine with silver-blue foliage. Needs curbing from spreading into surrounding plants, starving them of moisture. Do this at least once a year.

19. *Chamaecyparis pisifera* 'Plumosa Aurea Nana'. A bright yellow conifer. Needs rather similar conditions to *C. pisifera* 'Boulevard' but not quite so fussy. Can also be trimmed. Alternative for dry alkaline soils: a) *Thuja plicata* 'Stoneham Gold', irregular habit, or b) *Thuja occidentalis* 'Sunkist', golden year round, pyramidal habit.

20. *Euonymus radicans* 'Emerald Gaiety'. Dwarf, ground covering, variegated shrub. Trim each spring.

21. *Chamaecyparis pisifera* 'Filifera Nana'. Thread like, green foliage, rounded habit. Trim sides occasionally.

22. *Erica carnea* 'King George'. One of the oldest and most reliable winter flowering heathers. Pink.

23. *Thuja orientalis* 'Aurea Nana'. Golden yellow foliage in summer, more bronzed in winter.

24. *Juniperus horizontalis* 'Glauca'. The carpet juniper. Each May trim back the previous year's long shoots to promote a more dense habit of growth.

25. *Erica cinerea* 'Pink Ice'. Slow-growing, cushion-shaped, summer flowering bell heather. Will require a light trim each spring. Dislikes lime. Alternatives: a) *Erica carnea* 'Springwood Pink', prostrate, winter flowering heather, or b) *Helianthemum* 'Firedragon', silver-foliaged, flame coloured flowered shrub. The latter will also need trimming in March each year.

26. *Calluna vulgaris* 'Golden Carpet'. Golden-foliaged heather. Needs trimming each spring. Dislikes lime. Alternatives: a) *Erica carnea* 'Ann Sparkes', orange yellow foliaged, purple red flowered winter heather, or b) *Thymus* 'Golden Dwarf', non flowering dwarf, semi-shrubby thyme.

27. *Juniperus taxifolia* var. *lutchuensis* (syn. *maritima*). A ground-hugging green-foliaged juniper. Will need some pruning each year to prevent too wide a spread. Alternative *Juniperus procumbens* 'Nana' with similar habit.

28. *Sempervivum* 'Othello'. A houseleek with large, deep red rosettes. Alternative *Sempervivum* 'Mahogany' or any other red.

Three years later.

29. *Juniperus chinensis* 'Pyramidalis'. Steel blue, pyramidal habit, becomes quite large in time. Should be sprayed at the same time as *Picea* 'Albertiana Conica' since rather susceptible to red spider attack. Alternative *J. scopulorum* 'Gray Gleam', narrow pencil shape, grey blue foliage, slow growing.

30. *Phlox subulata* 'Temiscaming'. Prostrate alpine phlox, red flowers in spring. Trim back to prevent encroachment into base of conifers.

31. *Thuja occidentalis* 'Holmstrup'. Upright, pyramidal, slow-growing conifer, green in summer, slightly bronze-green in winter. Alternative *Juniperus chinensis* 'Robusta Green'.

Bed C

This planting was, I think, perhaps the most successful of all, using a combination of conifers, heathers, dwarf shrubs and ground cover. All plants almost without exception grew well and achieved at the end of three growing seasons almost a complete coverage. Some, as we have seen in earlier pages, needed curbing to prevent them growing into each other.

The ground cover items covered the hard straight edges of the wall, giving a more informal and natural look.

List of plants used in bed C

All plants are lime tolerant unless stated otherwise.

1. *Juniperus sabina* 'Tamariscifolia'. Prostrate conifer, excellent ground cover. Occasionally suffers from wilt and die-back. Prune away. Also prune to keep from spreading too wide in future years. Alternatives: a) *Juniperus sabina* 'Buffalo', or b) *Juniperus horizontalis* 'Banff'.

2. *Thuja orientalis* 'Conspicua'. Upright golden conifer. Alternative *Thuja occidentalis* 'Yellow Ribbon' or *T.o.* 'Sunkist'.

3. *Thuja occidentalis* 'Smaragd'. Originated in Denmark. Also known as *T.o.* 'Emerald', a translation of its Danish name. Also used for the hedge. Alternatives: a) *Juniperus communis* 'Sentinel' or b) *Pinus sylvestris* 'Fastigiata'.

4. *Taxus baccata* 'Repens Aurea'. Semi-prostrate golden foliaged yew, drooping branches. May need some trimming to keep from spreading in later years. Alternative *Thuja occidentalis* 'Golden Globe'.

5. *Hebe pinguifolia* 'Pagei'. Dwarf evergreen shrub. Grey-blue foliage, white flowers in May. Needs trimming to prevent encroachment into base of adjacent conifers. Can get straggly with age. Trim hard in early April to provide new shoots. Alternative *Juniperus horizontalis* 'Blue Chip'.

6. *Erica vagans* 'Mrs Maxwell'. Perhaps the best of the Cornish heaths. Rose-red flowers in late summer, early autumn. Will tolerate only slight amounts of lime. Alternatives for alkaline soils: a) *Erica carnea* 'Pink Spangles', pink winter flowering heather, or b) *Potentilla fruticosa* 'Red Ace', low growing shrub, red to orange flowers on and off from May until autumn frosts. Trim latter in March each year when established.

7. *Hedera helix* 'Chicago'. Excellent ground covering ivy. Needs trimming once, maybe twice each year to prevent growing into surrounding plants. Alternative *Vinca minor* Bowles variety, superior 'Periwinkle'.

8. *Erica carnea* 'Myretoun Ruby'. One of the best winter flowering heathers, masses of ruby-red flowers. Alternative *Erica carnea* 'Ruby Glow'.

9. *Chamaecyparis lawsoniana* 'Nana Albospica'. Slow growing conifer with white tipped foliage—sometimes slow to establish and may be prone to scorching of foliage in exposed situations. Alternative *Juniperus x media* 'Sulphur Spray', semi-prostrate conifer with creamy white foliage. The latter may need trimming in later years to prevent too wide a spread.

10. *Chamaecyparis lawsoniana* 'Blue Nantais'. Silver-blue foliaged upright conifer. Slow growing. Likely to be in short supply. Alternatives a) *Chamaecyparis lawsoniana* 'Chilworth Silver', or b) *Picea pungens* 'Globosa', dwarf blue spruce or c) *Picea pungens* 'Kosteri' or *Picea pungens*

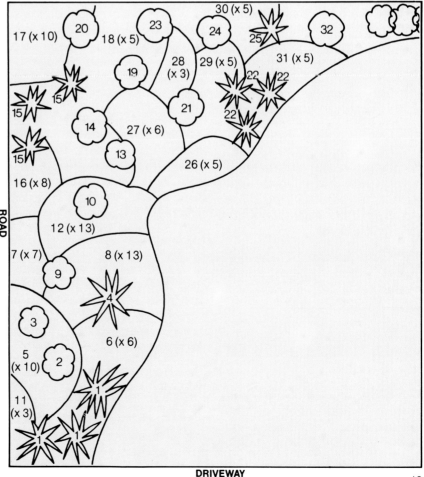

Bed C after planting in October.

Bed C after three seasons' growth.

'Hoopsii', both the latter, although slow growing may get too large in time, but could be pruned each March to keep shape and more moderate size (see photo page 45). All *Picea pungens* would need spraying with systemic insecticides.

11. *Hedera helix* 'Silver Queen'. Brightly variegated ivy with small leaves. Good ground cover. Trim back if it becomes too wide spreading. Alternative *Euonymus fortunei* 'Goldspot'.

12. *Erica carnea* 'Foxhollow'. Bright golden foliaged winter heather. Has few flowers. May have new shoots cut back by spring frosts, but will recover. Excellent foliage plant. May need trimming to prevent growing into base of conifers.

13. *Chamaecyparis obtusa* 'Nana Gracilis'. Dwarf form of the Hinoki cypress. Deep green glossy foliage. Very slow growing in early years.

14. *Thuja occidentalis* 'Lutescens'. Slow growing, upright conifer, pale creamy yellow foliage. Alternatives *Thuja occidentalis* 'Marrison Sulphur' may need trimming in later years.

15. *Juniperus horizontalis* 'Plumosa Compacta'. Semi-prostrate conifer, good for ground cover. May need pruning to prevent growing into other conifers and to prevent too wide a spread. Alternative *Juniperus horizontalis* 'Plumosa Youngstown' which is slightly more compact in habit.

16. *Euonymus fortunei* 'Variegatus'. Creeping variegated shrub will also climb walls. May need trimming to prevent growing into base of conifers. Alternative *E.f.* 'Emerald Gaiety'.

17. *Euonymus fortunei* 'Emerald 'n' Gold'. Green and golden variegated dwarf shrub. Will need trimming in later years to prevent encroachment into other plants.

18. *Berberis thunbergii* 'Atropur-

purea Nana'. A marvellous deciduous purple leaved dwarf shrub—and an excellent contrast plant. Alternative *B.t.* 'Baggatelle', similar but more compact.

19. *Juniperus scopulorum* 'Springbank'. A form of the Rocky Mountain juniper. Upright habit, silver-blue foliage. May need trimming each spring or early summer to improve density of the foliage. Alternatives a) *Juniperus scopulorum* 'Blue Heaven', similar but with coarser foliage, or b) *Juniperus scopulorum* 'Gray Gleam', denser in habit, narrow, grey-blue.

20. *Chamaecyparis lawsoniana* 'Ellwoodii'. Perhaps the best known and most popular garden conifer of all. Dislikes it too dry.

21. *Chamaecyparis pisifera* 'Filifera Aurea'. Slow growing conifer with a rounded, irregular habit and thread-like foliage. Light trimming will improve density and give it a more upright shape.

Golden year round. Alternative *Chamaecyparis pisifera* 'Gold Spangle', not so thread-like. Both have a tendency to scorch from frost, sun and wind in exposed positions in early years.

22. *Juniperus squamata* 'Blue Carpet'. First rate recently introduced prostrate conifer. Steel blue foliage. In this plan one plant would have been sufficient to cover area. Trimming leading branches to prevent too wide a spread will be necessary (see photo page 34).

23. *Thuja occidentalis* 'Lutea Naña'. Good year round colour, eventually becoming quite large. Can be trimmed. Perhaps better and rather slower growing alternative would be *Thuja occidentalis* 'Sunkist', denser in habit and more golden.

24. *Cryptomeria japonica* 'Lobbii Nana'. Broad irregular-shaped conifer, green in summer, bronze in winter. May need some trimming to prevent ' too large a spread. Alternative *Thuja occidentalis* 'Danica'.

25. *Taxus baccata* 'Semperaurea'. Golden-leaved, semi-erect spreading yew. Good winter colour. Some pruning may be necessary in later years.

26. *Erica carnea* 'Springwood White'. One of the best winter flowering heathers. Bright green foliage and good ground cover. May need trimming to prevent growing into conifers.

27. *Erica darleyensis* 'Furzey' (syn. 'Cherry Stevens'). Dark green foliage, deep pink flowers from January until April. May need trimming to prevent growing into conifers. Trim in April or May. Alternative *Erica darleyensis* 'J. W. Porter'.

28. *Calluna vulgaris* 'H. E. Beale'. Favourite double pink summer flowering heather. Trim old flowering spikes fairly hard each spring. Not lime tolerant.

Bed C photographed three years after planting.

Alternatives for alkaline soils a) *Erica erigena* 'W. T. Rackliff', winter heather with white flowers, or b) *Spiraea japonica* 'Little Princess', dwarf shrub with pink flowers most of the summer.

29. *Erica vagans* 'Lyonesse'. Flowers, white in late summer. Needs trimming each spring as soon as new growth appears. Not lime tolerant. Alternatives for alkaline soils a) either *Spiraea japonica* 'Golden Princess', bright golden leaved shrub, or b) use *Potentilla fruticosa* 'Abbotswood', a deciduous shrub with white flowers. This will require trimming each March to prevent becoming too large.

30. *Erica* x *darleyensis* 'Arthur Johnson'. Flowers pink from late November until April. Quite vigorous growth. May need trimming after flowering to prevent from becoming too large and growing into conifers.

31. *Erica carnea* 'Vivellii'. Winter flowering heather. Rich bronze-green foliage in summer, carmine flowers.

32. *Picea pungens* 'Globosa'. A miniature blue spruce with irregular rounded habit. Bright silver-blue foliage the year round. Can be attacked by insect pests. Spray with a systemic insecticide twice within fourteen days in May, repeat later in summer as necessary.

Bed D

This bed served two main purposes. First to enclose the grass area with plants almost completely to create a natural garden scene, and second to break up the straight lines of the wall of the house. The soil here was rather light and poor and because it was sheltered from prevailing westerly winds which bring most rain, it tended to be rather dry.

Some plants were slow to establish; we even lost one or two heathers, but I think there is no doubt at the end of the three year period that the plants had given a good account of themselves. The *Pyracantha* 'Orange Glow' against the wall helped to create colour and some maturity.

List of plants used in bed D

1. *Taxus baccata* 'Standishii'. A rather choice, slow growing golden-foliaged fastigiate yew. If not immediately obtainable, worth leaving a space for it to fill later.

2. *Taxus baccata* 'Repandens'. Dark green, almost black leaves, semi-prostrate habit. Slow growing but may need trimming in later years.

3. *Juniperus sabina* 'Blue Danube'. Semi-prostrate conifer. Quite vigorous. Will need pruning to prevent growing too large. Alternative *Juniperus* x *media* 'Mint Julep', green foliage, similar habit.

4. *Juniperus* x *media* 'Old Gold'. An outstanding trouble-free juniper, semi-prostrate. Will need pruning in later years to prevent becoming too large. Alternative the similar *J.* x *m.* 'Gold Coast'.

5. *Tsuga canadensis,* 'Jeddeloh'. A graceful semi-prostrate hemlock with drooping branches. Dislikes dry, alkaline soils but will tolerate some lime. Alternatives a) *Thuja occidentalis* 'Recurva Nana', dwarf green, rounded conifer, or b)

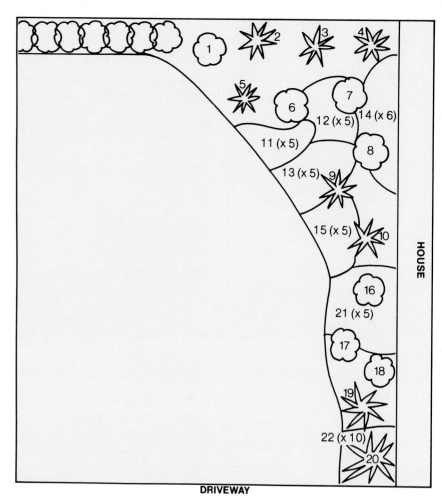

HOUSE

DRIVEWAY

Picea abies 'Nidiformis', flat-topped 'nest cypress'. The latter is one of the conifers which will need spraying against red spider mite.

6. *Chamaecyparis pisifera* 'Squarrosa Sulphurea'. Broad, dense bush with fine foliage, bright sulphur-yellow in summer. May need some trimming to prevent growing too wide and large.

7. *Juniperus scopulorum* 'Blue Heaven'. One of the bluest foliage conifers, particularly in summer. Rather open habit. Trimming sides in May each year will help to create denser habit. Alternatives *J.s.* 'Skyrocket' or *Pinus sylvestris* 'Fastigiata', an upright narrowly columnar 'Scots pine'.

8. *Chamaecyparis lawsoniana* 'Tamariscifolia'. A broad-spreading bright green conifer. Will eventually need some trimming to prevent

becoming too large. Possible alternative *Thuja occidentalis* 'Little Champion', a broad dome-shaped conifer becoming denser with age.

9. *Juniperus virginiana* 'Grey Owl'. Vigorous semi-prostrate juniper, smoky grey foliage. Perhaps too strong growing but can be kept in check for some years by annual pruning. Slower growing alternative *Juniperus virginiana* 'Silver Spreader', silver-blue foliage, more dense in habit.

10. *Taxus baccata* 'Summergold'. Semi-prostrate yew, golden foliage in summer. Vigorous shoots can be pruned back annually to keep plant to area and improve density. Alternative *Juniperus* x *media* 'Gold Coast'.

11. *Erica cinerea* 'Purple Beauty'. Summer flowering 'bell' heather. Will need light trim each spring when new shoots appear.

Not lime tolerant. Alternatives for alkaline soils a) *Erica darleyensis* 'J. W. Porter', purple-flowering winter heather, or b) *Campanula* 'Stella' a 'bellflower' with lavender-blue flowers all summer.

12. *Erica* x *darleyensis* 'Silberschmelze'. The name hides a first-class heather, flowers from January until April. May need some trimming to prevent encroachment into other plants. Alternative *E. carnea* 'Springwood White'.

13. *Erica* x *darleyensis* 'J.H. Brummage'. Golden foliage, pink flowers in winter. A good contrast plant.

14. *Hedera helix* 'Silver Queen'. Useful against a wall or as ground cover. Brightly variegated leaves, creeping habit. May need some trimming in later years to prevent growing into other plants. Alternative *Euonymus fortunei* 'Emerald Gaiety'.

15. *Erica carnea* 'Myretoun Ruby'. So good, included at both ends of the garden.

16. *Thuja occidentalis* 'Smaragd'. Also used again because of its neat habit and bright green foliage, making a pleasant contrast against the light-coloured brick and surrounding plants.

17. *Thuja plicata* 'Stoneham Gold'. Slow-growing, irregular-branched upright conifer. Good winter colour.

18. *Juniperus scopulorum* 'Skyrocket'. Narrow pencil-like form, blue-green foliage. Occasional opening up of branches due to snow, etc. These can either be tied back or trimmed off.

19. *Juniperus procumbens* 'Nana'. An excellent ground-hugging juniper, bright, apple-green foliage. May need some pruning in future years.

20. *Juniperus* x *media* 'Sulphur

Part of Bed D in late winter following autumn planting.

The same view three growing seasons after planting.

Spray'. This has replaced the original *J.* x *m.* 'Old Gold' which can still be used if preferred. 'Sulphur Spray' has creamy white foliage, semi-prostrate habit. May need some trimming in later years.

21. *Erica carnea* 'Springwood Pink'. Reliable, flat-growing, winter flowering heather.

22. *Ajuga reptans* 'Burgundy Glow'. Multi-coloured leaves, useful ground cover, light blue, spiky flowers in May. Can seed itself and become untidy. Trim and replant as necessary.

Conifer hedges

Conifers are nearly all evergreens and that, of course, is why so many of them are useful for hedges and screens—giving you privacy, shelter and form and structure to the garden. There are of course evergreen trees or shrubs suitable for hedges such as the hollies, but the range of heights, colours and textures of foliage among the conifers gives an unequalled range.

When selecting a conifer for a hedge try first to decide what you want it to do for you. Do you need it to give you shelter from strong winds from whatever direction? Do you need it for privacy or because you just think it will look nice? How quickly do you want it to grow? Before you say, 'I want it to grow one metre a year and then stop after two years', I can tell you you are asking for the impossible. There are conifers that will grow one metre a year, but without trimming they will keep on growing one metre a year for nearly thirty years.

A conifer hedge that grows quickly is very useful but will need constant attention to keep it to the required height and once it is over $2\text{-}2\frac{1}{2}$m (6-8ft) it becomes quite a job to keep under control.

As a general guide, a fast growing conifer makes an ideal hedge or screen for the larger garden but is less suitable for the smaller one. Here it would be advisable to go for something slower growing which will take longer to reach $2\text{-}2\frac{1}{2}$m if that is what you want, but which will be less trouble and work in years to come.

Here are a few suggestions for conifer hedges:

Note the string drawn out as a planting guide. The piece of wood is used to obtain equal spacing between the plants.

Mixing peat in the hole ready for the next conifer. Peat helps the growth of new roots, as most container plants are grown in peat-based compost.

Placing the conifer in the hole. The plant is set slightly deeper than the compost level in the pot.

The hedge three years after planting. It can be trimmed at the sides but will not need stopping until 1.5m (5ft).

Fast growing conifers

Cupressocyparis leylandii, the most popular hedging plant in Britain, will grow 8-10m (25-30ft) in ten years, and ultimately 25-30m (75-90ft). Space 60-75cm (24-30in) apart when planting, perhaps 100cm (3ft) if using large plants. Trim twice a year in April and July or August. There is a more compact, and slower growing form with golden foliage *Cupressocyparis* 'Castlewellan Gold'. This should not need so much trimming.

Thuja plicata the western red cedar and its particularly improved form *T.p.* 'Atrovirens' are much hardier for more extreme climates and both make superb hedges. They are excellent for heavier soils and have the advantage of making new growth from bare wood—an attribute that few other conifers can claim. Space 60-75cm (24-30in) apart. *T. plicata* is often produced from seed and can be variable for hedging. Trim sides when hedge reaches 150cm (5ft) in April and July or August. The variety *T.p.* 'Atrovirens' has a rather neater habit.

Medium growing conifers

Chamaecyparis lawsoniana, the

Lawson cypress, and its faster growing varieties make good hedges, but can have a tendency to go bare at the base unless kept completely clear of vegetation 30cm (1ft) away from the outside of the hedge. They are hardy throughout most of Britain but not in climates that have prolonged hard winters. They also tend to get windburn from cold winds in winter. *C. lawsoniana* is often offered as seedlings and may be variable in colour and growth. Why not try *C.l.* 'Lane' or *C.l.* 'Dutch Gold', both attractive golden leaved forms or *C.l.* 'Pembury Blue'? All grow approximately 2.5-3m (8-10ft) in ten years, ultimately 15-25m (45-75ft).

Forms of the English yew *Taxus baccata* or the Japanese yew *Taxus cuspidata* make reasonable hedges, particularly in formal situations and are quite amenable to trimming, July and August being good months. According to the variety, plant 60-75cm (24-30in) apart.

Although one could suggest other conifers for hedging, one of the most useful and adaptable is *Thuja occidentalis,* the white cedar and its forms. Here are extremely hardy varieties with green and golden foliage, growing well on a wide range of soils. I chose (for Mr and Mrs Edens' garden) the variety raised in Denmark with the almost unpronounceable name of *T.o.* 'Smaragd' (which, translated, means emerald) and it has proved itself an outstanding hardy conifer, both as a specimen and as a hedge. Its height after ten years can be expected to be 2.5-3m (8-10ft) and ultimately perhaps 8-10m (25-30ft) but it can be kept at 1.5-2m (4-6½ft) indefinitely if required. Space 45-60cm (18-24in). It needs little trimming but trim top when at required height. Other forms worth considering are *T.o.* 'Europe Gold', 'Yellow Ribbon'

Trimming the top of a hedge of *Thuya occidentalis* 'Smaragd'.

A fine hedge of *Cupressocyparis leylandii* 'Castlewellan'.

or 'Sunkist' all with golden foliage, and *T.o.* 'Holmstrup' or *T.o.* 'Pyramidalis', both green in summer but bronzing in winter.

When you are planting the hedge, the same preparation rules apply as for other plants: clear perennial weeds, dig thoroughly, mixing in well rotted compost or peat. Detailed instruction is given here in photographs and captions.

Making the most of the lawn

After spiking, the best way to maintain the texture of the soil is by topdressing with peat. This is worked into the holes with the back of a rake.

To develop and maintain a perfect lawn is both costly and time-consuming and sometimes extremely frustrating! Most home-owners with a garden are content to have a lawn which looks healthy and an attractive green, complementing the plants and surroundings and, at the same time, fairly hard–wearing.

This really is what was required in the Edens' garden, but when we started, the lawn certainly fell a long way short of being green and healthy. Being no expert myself, I asked Fisons if they would give us some advice and help to try to resurrect the lawn. Their immediate reaction was to suggest either re-sowing or, better, re-turfing, since the lawn contained many weeds, and was in a rather bad condition.

However, they were willing to try to improve its condition and appearance, which they without doubt achieved with the help of George and Angela Edens. What follows on these two pages is some general advice on how to improve and maintain your lawn to a reasonable standard.

Do not expect miracles, but take note of the various points mentioned which go to produce a reasonable lawn—yours may suffer from bad drainage, not enough light or a great many other factors. Certainly following some of the basic points mentioned below will help you improve your lawn (unless you have already achieved a perfect sward).

Regular care and maintenance are important if the lawn is to be kept looking its best. Important points are regular mowing, regular feeding, the occasional topdressing, plus frequent aeration, rolling and watering.

Mowing

Regular mowing is important as this controls the coarser grasses, helps fine grass to produce a dense sward, and discourages weeds.

Grass cuttings should always be removed, otherwise, if they are left to form a matted layer, the turf will deteriorate through lack of light, air and water. Mow at least once a week from April to October, and more frequently when the grass is growing fast. Cut once or twice during the winter when conditions are suitable. Vary the direction of mowing from time to time to ensure even cutting all over, and set the cutting blades 18mm ($\frac{3}{4}$in) for most lawns. This height should be increased by about 6mm ($\frac{1}{4}$in) in autumn and winter.

It is important never to 'scalp' grass by cutting it too short in an attempt to save work, as this will damage and gradually weaken the grass plants.

To give a lawn the well-groomed look the edges should be trimmed every time the lawn is cut.

Feeding

Starved lawns quickly become covered in weeds and moss, while the grass goes pale and dies away to leave ugly, bare patches. Regular feeding is essential to add colour and quality to a lawn, enabling it to develop a dense, deep green carpet.

The essential ingredients for such healthy growth are nitrogen, phosphates, and potassium, and are to be found in most of the ready compounded lawn fertilizers. Apply in late March or April (preferably with one of the wheeled spreaders to ensure accuracy of distribution) and repeat in May or July. Water freely if the weather is dry. Where weeds are troublesome use a combined fertilizer and weedkiller instead. Finally, in September or October apply an autumn lawn food to rejuvenate the lawn after

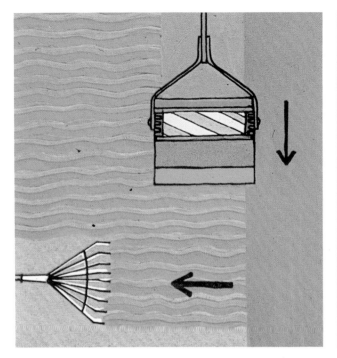

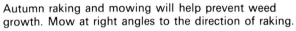

Autumn raking and mowing will help prevent weed growth. Mow at right angles to the direction of raking.

Using a sharp spade to cut a clean edge. Pull out any weeds and grass and clear away.

heavy summer use and encourage good root growth through the difficult winter months.

Aeration, raking and topdressing

All important operations that are well worth undertaking if good, steady, healthy growth is to be maintained.

A light raking with a special lawn rake can be done every three to four weeks during spring and summer, and then more vigorously in September to drag out partially decaying debris. Vary the direction of raking to raise straggling grasses and weeds into the path of the mower.

Should the lawn become compacted through heavy use during the summer months this can result in thinning of the grass and invasion by weeds and moss.

The solution is to aerate the surface to a depth of 8-10cm (3-4in) by spiking with a hollow-tined fork or even an ordinary garden fork. After piercing the lawn apply a topdressing of peat and with the back of a garden rake rub it well into the surface and the holes,

taking care not to leave any grass covered. Dressings like this can also be used to even out any dips and hollows.

Finally—and perhaps this is the most obvious thing to be neglected—do ensure there is an adequate supply of water from April to September, otherwise your green sward will turn to brown.

Making a new lawn

If you have a new garden or your lawn is really so bad that you feel you should remake it, then you will need to start from scratch. Here again is some basic advice on how to go about it.

Preparation

With all gardens, the first consideration is to examine the soil, but whatever the soil, from the coarse grained sandy through to the fine-textured, sticky clay, the basic treatment needs are the same; having thoroughly dug the ground over and removed all perennial weed and roots into the top 7.5-10cm (3-4in) of soil apply a soil conditioning material at the rate of about 2.5kg per sq m

(6½lb per sq yd). The purpose of this is to improve the soil structure and allow an improved movement of air and water. The next operation is to then tread the surface, walking lengthwise and crosswise so that every part of the area is evenly firm. Finally, it should then be raked level, removing any large stones, to produce a nice, even surface. Before sowing or turfing a lawn it is advisable to apply a fertilizer. Use an autumn lawn food (these are not too high in nitrogen) a day or two before at the rate of 50g per sq m (2oz per sq yd) and finish off with another raking.

Seed is the cheapest method of producing a lawn and does permit the selection of grasses to suit the site and purpose. Turf provides the quickest way of producing a reasonable lawn—but can contain undesirable grasses and weeds. Turf can be laid at any time of the year when the soil is crumbly and moist, although the best times are early spring and autumn. The two most favourable periods for sowing seed are during April or September.

The garden grows

We started in September and by October Mr and Mrs Edens' front garden was complete. The informal shape of the borders had been made to break up the straight lines all around to try to create a 'natural' garden in a suburban setting. Most of the hard work had been completed and now it was a question of waiting for the plants to grow and the garden to mature.

Year round colour

The boast of year round colour using conifers and heathers is not an idle one and although in the first autumn and winter the plants were not large enough to make a tremendous impact, colour there

The eight-year-old 'old garden' of Mr and Mrs Edens before replanting.

The garden immediately after replanting, and looking rather sparse.

A year after planting. Some growth has been made although the grass is very patchy.

Nearly three years after planting and a lot of growth has taken place.

certainly was. It continued quite dry into the autumn but then rain and some frosts came, immediately creating different hues among the conifers and generally deepening the colour effect. This was heightened from late November onwards when the winter flowering heathers started coming into bloom. By late February nearly all were in full flower and made a very bright impression. A survey of other gardens on the housing estate showed that comparisons could be made between these and the Edens' garden even in that first winter.

The complete garden in the March following planting.

Two years on and some cheerful colours after a hard winter.

Work load
I think the Edens would not deny that for the first winter there was practically nothing to do in the garden with the exception of an occasional seedling weed to be pulled up. The peat mulch had done its work in preventing a whole crop of weed seed from germinating.

Unfortunately the well-prepared soil and particularly the peat had attracted one or two of the local cats who found it somewhat irresistible! Little damage was done but dogs and cats can be a problem when a young garden on an open plan scheme is becoming established. Dogs in particular can render young plants unsightly so they should be kept at a distance. There is a proprietary chemical spray which is a deterrent and I believe quite effective, (see advice on page 76).

Autumn planting
Although one can safely plant container grown plants at any time of the year, early autumn planting of evergreens still has many advantages. The soil is still warm and plants have an opportunity to form new roots before the onset of winter. These fresh feeding roots will enable the plant to draw moisture from the

The Edens' garden three years after planting, photographed in the early autumn sunlight. Compare with the late winter views above.

soil the following spring when cold, easterly winds often dry out evergreen and conifer leaves and lead to browning of foliage and sometimes complete loss. This is much more likely, however, to occur with plants from open ground than those in containers which should have their own self-contained root system.

In the spring
Little did we know what weather was in store for us later in the

summer—just as well that we had managed to get the garden planted early the previous autumn.

Towards the end of March when there was still plenty of flower on the winter heathers, new growth was beginning on the summer flowering types. This is the time to trim back these, the *Erica cinerea*, *vagans* and of course the lings, *Calluna vulgaris* and cultivars. Although the plants were small and had only a few shoots, these were trimmed with shears by Mrs Edens to make them bush out and create more flower spikes for the summer. More detail on the subject of trimming comes later.

Weeding
This was not an onerous task in the first year but important enough. A heather and conifer garden can be weed free with relatively little work—as long as perennial weeds are first eradicated. After that it is a question of pulling out new seedling weeds as soon as they appear. Seedlings are easier to pull out at the young stage, particularly where the soil is friable and moist. If it is necessary to step between the plants when wet and the soil becomes compacted, just prick up again with the prongs of a fork.

There is more space between the plants in the first season after planting than there will be in subsequent years so there is more area for seeds to germinate. Consequently expect more weeding in the first years although it would be surprising if it amounted to as much as half an hour a week. As the heathers grow and spread they will gradually become effective ground cover and weed suppressants.

Although hoeing may seem a less backaching and simpler alternative in keeping weeds under control I advise against the use of a hoe. Some conifers and nearly all heathers are surface rooting and the blade of a hoe will certainly damage these roots.

The summer after planting
The record books were changed in many places in Britain and Europe following one of the warmest, driest summers since records began.

Although gardeners are aware of the weather and its effect on their plants, this summer posed

Bed C from the house showing the importance of winter colour.

problems seldom encountered before with desperate water shortages and even water rationing in some parts of the country.

It was a difficult year for a newly planted garden. First sprinklers were banned in the district and then hoses. Water was brought by watercart on two occasions to prevent losses through drought. But on the whole the plants fared better than expected—the peat mulch being a definite help in retaining moisture. There were the inevitable losses—perhaps half a dozen heathers, one conifer—but we, like every gardener, were relieved to see the rain when it arrived in autumn.

By October the first anniversary of planting had arrived and although there hadn't appeared to be much progress during the summer, growth was certainly noticeable by autumn. The hot summer had produced early ripened wood and berry fruits everywhere. The heathers in the garden were no exception: flower buds appearing early on the winter flowering types, promising

a splash of colour in the winter.

The lawn had brightened up considerably after the autumn rains but when the rains came they didn't seem to want to stop.

Work in the garden
Practically no work was necessary during the second autumn and winter beyond keeping a few weeds under control. The few plants that had not survived the summer drought were replaced and those that had looked a little unhappy seemed to pull round once the rains came.

Trimming the edges
One job which should be checked properly at least once a year is the edging. When the garden was first planted the edges of the lawn were neatly cut away with a spade and to a depth of 5-8cm (2-3in). This enabled a pair of edging shears or ordinary garden shears to be easily used to trim the grass when it grew again in the spring and keep the lawn looking neat and tidy. It is important to keep this edge between grass and soil at the stated depth to prevent grasses growing into the border and to allow room

to make trimming easier. Soil naturally falls into this cleft reducing the depth and allowing grass to grow back. Try to keep this from happening by going round it once a year with a spade to push out the soil and keep the grass and weeds in place.

Three years on

The three years over which this garden developed were fascinating. Nearly every year there seems to be some weather out of the normal, hot or cold, wet or dry. If the first summer was one of the driest for years, the second winter was one of the coldest, with prolonged frost and snow. So, although all climates are relative, the conifers and heathers had to withstand some considerable tests. While summer flowering heathers and some shrubs looked decidedly 'browned off', they would recover when growth began after a very late spring. The *Erica carnea* and *Erica darleyensis* types bloomed through it all. One gardener in Ontario, Canada, informed me that when they have an early start to their normally hard winter the winter flowering heathers do not come into flower until snows and ice melt in March. As one might imagine, it is just as though they were in a cold store.

By the time the three years were over, the small plants in the Edens' garden had gradually increased to a quite respectable size and the overall scene was one showing much more in the way of plants than soil. The more vigorous heathers, as can be seen from the photographs, had spread to create a colourful and interesting patchwork, with conifers, shrubs and alpines providing accent and interest.

The importance of winter colour

Many gardens can be a depressing sight in winter. The normal range of deciduous

The whole garden in late winter, 2½ years after planting.

shrubs, roses and trees have very little to say for themselves from November until April—in the case of roses, until June. Even the standard range of conifers often seen in gardens have a dull tone throughout the winter. None of this is necessary. The conifers and heathers in Mr and Mrs Edens' garden make a bright show on winter and early spring days when a touch of colour is needed after a dull, dark winter. Winter colour, to my mind, is of paramount importance in the garden and although this season is not the time when most people want or can consider gardening, an area of conifers, heathers, shrubs with attractive foliage or stems, which

can be seen from the house or on your way to the garage or street, can be of continual interest and enjoyment. Winter flowering heathers being generally hardier than summer flowering types —with the exception of callunas—and also lime tolerant, are an obvious choice.

Conifers with different coloured foliage, golds, greens and blues, and various forms, firs, pines and spruces—add an extra ingredient if planted in association. How cheerful to see such a display of varied colour during or after a long winter.

A ten-year backward glance

It's a funny thing, time. When you are ten years old, the idea of looking ten years ahead is almost incomprehensible—and those ten years probably seem the longest of your life. As you get older, ten years becomes a smaller proportion of your life—but they always seem much longer in anticipation than in retrospect. So it is and has been with Mr and Mrs Edens' garden and because this was a finite thing, it is extremely useful to measure a ten-year period.

The objective achieved?

It is certainly true to say that George and Angela Edens (who still consider themselves reluctant gardeners) have been delighted with their garden, as have many others who have copied some of the ideas. They have had a show of colour the year round with almost no time spent on the garden between October and March. On average, apart from the grass cutting, they spend less than half an hour a week in the summer on maintenance. They admit that if they wanted perfection, they could and should have spent more time in trimming and spraying in summer to ward off pests, and given an occasional watering. They have lost a few conifers and have had to replace two or three of them. The *Picea glauca* 'Albertiana Conica', the dwarf Alberta spruce, always prone to red spider mite, now looks a beautiful specimen: it is encouraging that it has completely recovered from being defoliated two or three years previously. The *Juniperus scopulorum* 'Blue Heaven' and 'Springbank' have gone somewhat thin at the base, due, I think, to not being trimmed regularly enough, and from overcrowding by other plants.

The advantages of pruning

The Edens have been quite

Ten years on. Compare the garden with the photographs on page 28.

zealous at times in their trimming, keeping heathers from spoiling specimen conifers. Trimming should be done as soon as heathers or other plants start to crowd against the foliage. Cut back with shears or secateurs in early spring and again in mid summer each year. Eventually you may decide that because the specimen conifer has increased its outward growth, the plants can be allowed to intertwine. This does look natural but remember that if the conifer cannot get light and air on its foliage it will go brown.

That will not be noticeable until you remove the heather growing into it—which may never be necessary, of course.

On other pages there are many details showing how to prune conifers—and without doubt it is often an advantage and sometimes a necessity to do so (see pages 34, 35 and 42 and 43). It is ironical, perhaps, that, to start with, you can't wait for your plants to grow and when they do, you have to trim and prune to keep them in check. But this will improve the plants and enhance their appearance if it is done carefully and at the right time of the year.

Successes and failures

The Edens' garden site is essentially a rather dry one, particularly in summer. This, together with the obvious congestion in some of the planting, has resulted in some plants which normally require more moisture looking a little thin and starved. One or two of the summer flowering heathers, for instance, have struggled and should have been replaced by other plants. But, apart from an occasional loss, I think this garden has proved that it *is* possible to have a year round garden, requiring little or no maintenance.

A suburban site, of course, is open not only to your own dogs and cats but also your neighbours'. In the early years local pets were somewhat troublesome, but as the garden became more mature the plants stood up for themselves and even though the occasional spoiling of a conifer occurred, this was not generally too noticeable. The Edens' cat has now found itself one or two nice warm spots in the garden in which to sun itself undisturbed by other animals.

It is interesting to look again at a photograph of the Edens' original garden. It is I'm afraid, a good representation of a traditional British suburban garden.

Of course no blame should fall upon anyone whose garden fits the traditional, and perhaps rather unimaginative, mould. But I hope that some of the ideas we had for Mr and Mrs Edens' garden will, in time, benefit others. Showing by example is the best way of passing on gardening tips. For myself, I am grateful to George and Angela Edens, for this welcome opportunity to put ideas into practice.

The garden ten years after planting. Compare with page 31.

The garden from the path.

Maintaining the garden

The art of keeping a garden attractive and its plants in good shape is to try to follow the old adage 'prevention is better than cure'.

I think that all gardeners and even non-gardeners would agree that keeping the grass cut and the weeds under control is a basic essential in achieving an attractive garden setting. But when it comes to plants—particularly those with which one is not familiar—what should be done to achieve the best results?

Keeping the plants in good shape

Both heathers and many conifers can be improved by pruning or trimming. If your garden is small it will, on some conifers, be essential to prune to prevent them outgrowing their allotted area. Some trimming will be necessary in later years.

I make no excuse for some repetition on the subject of pruning conifers and heathers. It is a subject about which the general gardening public seems to have little knowledge or understanding, and yet, as plants grow, it is basic common sense to get them to adapt somewhat to the garden—to make the most of them as garden plants. On the next few pages I deal with the general matter of trimming and pruning and follow some of the work which was carried out in the Edens' garden in the first three years. On page 42 is more detailed coverage on pruning some specialist conifers.

Both conifers and heathers should be pruned from a fairly early age, probably one or two years after planting, but this will be

Trimming growths of *Juniperus squamata* 'Blue Carpet' to keep it in check.

according to the particular variety. Heathers are dealt with on the next two pages. Many of the dwarfer, more compact-growing conifers may never need pruning, but those that are untidy in habit and more vigorous in growth certainly will benefit from it. Take the semi-prostrate *Juniperus virginiana* 'Grey Owl' for instance, an attractive grey-foliaged form, ideal for banks and ground cover. Without pruning, in the ten years it has been in the Edens' garden it would have spread 3-4m (10-13ft). By regular pruning of side shoots this can happily be kept to 1 metre (3ft).

You might not think it necessary, perhaps, to control dwarf shrubs and alpines. But some attention is required over the first few years, depending on the types of plant, if you want to get the best out of them. For instance, *Euonymus* 'Emerald

Gaiety' and 'Emerald 'n' Gold', *Hebe* and even the creeping ivies are best trimmed every other year at least in a garden such as this. It will improve their neatness and appearance and prevent them from invading the specimen conifers. As for the alpines, the types used in the Edens' garden are basically the stronger growing carpeting forms such as ajugas and acaena and alpine phlox, *(P. subulata)*. They can grow very quickly and will need restraining if they are not to invade other plants' territory. It is possible that later they may die out in patches and need replanting with younger, more vigorous shoots.

Pruning

Either April, late July or early August are the best times for conifer pruning (and also for conifer hedge trimming). Why? Well, April is just before new

Trimming irregular shoots from *Chamaecyparis pisifera* 'Boulevard'.

to disguise the cut. The juniper should not suffer if it is a clean cut and will soon cover up the area with new growth as long as brown or dead looking foliage has not been exposed.

Conifers and heathers, though relatively trouble-free, may have problems which can make the plants look unsightly and sometimes eventually lead to their death.

There are very few rules of thumb to follow and it may often be after the cause of the problem has come and gone that the results are evident.

Therefore, one should be able to identify probable causes and take preventive measures where problems are likely to occur. I think most of the areas likely to be of general concern arose at one time or another in George and Angela Edens' garden. How we coped with the problems will perhaps serve as a guide as to what might be expected for any gardener growing the same type of plants.

growth is made in early summer, quickly covering over new cuts, and July will have seen much early growth which can be trimmed, leaving time for more growth to be made and wounds to be healed.

All that is necessary in the way of tools is a sharp pair of secateurs. The older and thicker the stem to be pruned, the sharper should be the tool and the more strength applied. On very old plants, with thicker and tougher stems, it may be necessary to use a pruning saw.

Some semi-prostrate conifers do get to very large proportions if left untrimmed in this case one often has to be quite brutal and trim back as much as 60 or 90cm (2-3ft). Try to prune just under a small branchlet which should help

Cutting back ivy to prevent it growing into the base of the thuja.

35

Trimming *Erica vagans* 'Lyonesse'. Trimming helps to keep plants young and healthy.

Clearing *Acaena buchananii* from the base of the heathers by cutting it with a spade, then lifting with a fork.

Cultural causes

Let it be said that soil type and conditions, weather etc., all have a bearing on the way plants behave and some plants are more susceptible to different conditions than others.

Some of the conifers, such as *Chamaecyparis pisifera* 'Boulevard', are adversely affected by conditions which are too dry. They are prone to go rather brown in patches and unless given ample water and possibly trimmed will be unlikely to improve greatly.

This cultivar, though a beautiful slow growing conifer in favourable conditions, tends to be a little fussy, requiring good drainage, yet ample moisture in summer to give of its best.

Nice to report that the specimen shown in the photograph improved considerably with the treatment advised, and with regular pruning made a

beautiful plant at ten years old.

Pest or disease

Sometimes dieback of branches will occur on junipers. Occasionally pests attack the plants in spring or summer and are usually gone before anything looks wrong. Some are prone to fungal diseases which may cause wilting or dieback of branches. Do not get too alarmed as this is not likely to be a usual or regular occurrence but the effects can be unsightly. Pruning off the offending branch or branches will usually cure the problem which may not recur. If dieback continues to be a problem a fungicidal spray used both in early spring and late summer should help. Spray twice within two weeks at each period.

Trimming heathers

Although some of the heather enthusiasts do not trim or prune,

preferring the more natural look, I think it essential to do so. The plants are kept younger, neater in appearance and almost invariably flower more profusely with regular trimming.

As can be seen, trimming should take place on summer flowering heathers whilst the winter flowering types are still in flower, i.e. late March or early April. One should wait until little shoots appear on last year's stems. The purists might say secateurs should be used but they can make it a very long job and I suggest a sharp pair of garden shears as adequate for the task.

If heathers are regularly trimmed they can be cut fairly hard back but care should be taken not to go too far back into old wood since new shoots may not appear. However, one should be able to at least prune back most of the previous year's

Forking up the compacted soil after trimming and prior to mulching. This allows air to get to the roots.

Mulching to a depth of 3–5cm (1½–2in) with peat. Make sure the peat goes under the edges of the heathers.

growth without causing damage. It is often amazing how much new vigorous and healthy growth can be obtained by such good husbandry.

Winter flowering heathers will seldom, if ever, need trimming unless they need to be kept within bounds or become untidy. Immediately after flowering, i.e. April or early May is usually the best time for this. This certainly applies to *Erica carnea* varieties, which are more compact than *E. x darleyensis* types.

Hedge trimming

Thuja occidentalis 'Smaragd' was chosen for the short stretch of hedge because it is relatively slow growing and the required height of 1.5-2m (5-6ft) could be maintained without detriment to the plants.

The hedge was not trimmed for three years after planting.

After that a light trim on the sides was all that was necessary and each season from now on it should be trimmed and will fill in some more.

Mulching

After two and a half years the original sedge peat mulch had thinned somewhat and the soil had in places become compacted. It seemed a good idea to aerate the soil by forking and give a further mulch. Finish the spring pruning first so that there is no need to tread on the garden again for perhaps some months.

Sedge peat, sphagnum peat or even well-composted bark will serve as a mulch. None is cheap—probably none absolutely necessary but all will be beneficial to your garden.

Summer growth

After trimming and mulching and

despite any cold, late springs the garden really begins to make growth. Root systems become firmly established and, with plenty of spring rainfall, conifers, heathers and shrubs start into a new lease of life.

The quietest period for flower for the heather family is the late spring. I had put in some dwarf shrubs and some alpines for ground cover, colour and variety. These helped to fill in the flowering gap although there was no lack of colour on the conifers and heathers since the various greens, blues and yellows of the foliage provided their own somewhat more muted display.

By late June the first flower appeared on the *Erica cinerea* varieties, continuing into July and August to be followed by the callunas and in September by the *Erica vagans*—much to look forward to.

Moving a large conifer

It may not be very often that one wishes to undertake what is a rather onerous task—moving a large conifer. However, it can be done successfully with plants of even up to 5m (16ft) or more—but at this size, of course, it is a job for the specialist, the nurseryman or landscape company.

If you think you can do most of the work yourself but will need a hand with the lifting, let your neighbour or a friend know, so that he or she is on hand at the critical time.

The point being, of course, that if so much work is involved you must be sure firstly that you want to move the conifer, and secondly that having made the effort you want the move to be successful. Below, are shown all of the stages involved to ensure the basis of success.

Why move? Well, perhaps your conifers are too close and will spoil in future years. Or maybe you think one of them is in the wrong position and is eventually going to get too large if left where it is.

Of course, all conifers will not be as ideally situated for access as the one I moved below—you may

Start by cutting a circle roughly 30cm (12in) away from the base of the trunk. Increase for larger plants.

Make a trench wide enough for the width of a spade. Dig all round, severing the roots.

Loose soil at top should be eased away to lessen weight and prevent rootball splitting.

The plant is now almost on a pedestal. Make sure all tap roots are cut and the plant is nearly ready to move.

Ease plant backwards and insert hessian sacking or polythene sheet beneath the plant from one side.

Move plant in opposite direction and pull hessian through. Try not to let the rootball crack.

have plants growing very close to the base. These, if possible, should also be moved, if only temporarily, otherwise it will be difficult to make the trench necessary to get a good rootball. It is probably advisable also to use an anti-desiccant a few days prior to lifting (see page 40), and make sure the specimen has been well watered if the weather conditions are dry.

Root pruning

If you have time to delay the move it may pay to root prune or undercut some months before, i.e. in March and then move the plant in October. This would mean going to about stage 3 and then filling the soil back, perhaps using pure, moist peat against the cut roots. Keep well watered and new feeding roots will form before autumn and the move is likely to

have a better chance of success.

The plant shown being moved is *Chamaecyparis lawsoniana* 'Allumii Gold'. Chamaecyparis generally form good rootballs naturally and root pruning would not be so essential. Picea, pinus and to a lesser extent juniperus and taxus do not form good rootballs, so root pruning one season prior to moving would be definitely advisable.

Tie hessian tightly and wrap string round the rootball for extra security.

Take care when lifting to do it in easy stages. Get help if required.

Assess width for planting in grass. Prepare the planting hole first.

A good 30cm (12in) clearance should be allowed all round.

Mix peat and grit into the hole to achieve good friable soil conditions.

Assess depth of hole required. Plant slightly deeper than before.

Untie hessian. Some will rot if left, but remove it from the top of plant.

Make sure plant is in an upright position and firm loose soil.

Remove footprints with a fork. This helps to avoid panning of the soil.

A few other hints on moving a conifer

Some conifers may not move very easily or may not, hard as one tries, lift with a rootball. If necessary even more precautions can be taken:

a Prepare new planting area thoroughly beforehand. Make sure all tools are to hand.

b Spray with an anti-desiccant a few days before lifting. This will then be dry and protect the plant from loss of moisture during the moving operation.

c Give the plant a really good watering a few days before. This will at least ensure that it has taken up all available moisture and will help the move.

If a conifer is very tall or does not have a good rootball it will almost certainly require a supporting stake. This should be strong enough and of a length sufficient to go into the ground to a depth of at least 60cm (2ft). It should be carefully inserted fairly close to the plant, but not so close as to damage the roots. If possible a proper tree tie should be used (obtainable at garden centres, garden shops etc.,) otherwise polythene string. If this is used put a piece of sacking or cloth around the trunk of the tree first. The polythene string must be cut away after one season, otherwise it will cut into the stem and cause permanent damage.

If the plant is too broad or does not have an identifiable trunk or main stem, at least three stakes should be used further away from the plant and a band or stretch of hessian tied around the foliage and attached to the stakes. However, something similar to that shown (bottom right) with stronger stakes could be used both to break the wind and support the plant.

And, whatever happens, keep the plant well-watered in spring and summer, and on hot

Spray with an anti-desiccant which allows plant to breathe and prevents drying-out of foliage.

evenings spray the foliage—it all helps and will be an added insurance for successful transplanting.

Regular root pruning

Conifers that are likely to need moving in the foreseeable future may need root pruning. If you have a bed of dwarf conifers and they are likely to get too close in time, every second year, in April or September, just cut down with a sharp spade around the plant close to the outside of the foliage and to the depth of the spade. This will sever some of the major roots, encouraging the conifer to make fresh more fibrous ones and will by itself help that plant to make a compact root system for when you eventually wish to move it. It will slow down the growth of the plant slightly, but since you will not have dug a trench, or undercut the rootball, the plant is unlikely to feel any shock or damage. Afterwards water well if the weather is dry. This is a relatively easy and quick procedure.

Moving a small conifer

Small conifers generally move very easily, particularly if they have originally been planted with plenty of peat and root pruned regularly as outlined above. Depending on the size of the conifer it may or may not be necessary to dig a small trench around it prior to lifting. In the Edens' garden we needed to move a *Juniperus squamata* 'Blue Star' from the conifer bed since it was too close to the other two. Here are the stages we went through and which you should follow: (1) Cut down with the bottom edge of a spade close to the edge of the foliage, the spade slightly pointed towards the centre of the plant. Undercut to make sure the plant is free to lift and all roots have been severed. (2) Lift the plant on to the surface with the spade or carefully on to polythene or sacking. It is a good idea to use polythene sheeting to put the soil or the plant on so that it doesn't make a mess on the grass or surrounding plants. (3) Ease away with your hands any excess soil from the rootball, particularly near the top. This will lighten the weight and also help to avoid the rootball coming apart. Lift the plant carefully by hand into a barrow and move to new planting position. If you plan to plant the conifer in a permanent position in the garden soil preparation should have been completed. Planting can take place following the procedures outlined for moving a large conifer. It will probably not be necessary to protect a small conifer with a windbreak but an anti-dessicant spray will be beneficial.

Knock in stakes around the plant to support protective netting which will provide wind protection while the plant gets established.

Tie the netting or shading material to the stakes, making sure it does not touch the plant. This will further reduce risk of scorching.

Pruning conifers

When I first started growing conifers, I considered that it was entirely wrong to trim them, believing, rather as a purist, that it was somehow unnatural and that they should be allowed to develop their own character untouched by human hand. I have long since changed my mind.

There are many reasons for helping or changing nature—and as gardeners we all do it with any number of plants, so why not conifers? Hedges, of course, are normally trimmed but conifers grown in this way are not the only ones that can benefit from some form of training.

There are many reasons for pruning but to put it succinctly many conifers look much better for it, while others—and particularly the prostrate and semi-prostrate conifers—may soon get out of hand unless pruned from an early age. Pruning when plants are young can keep them denser in habit because it promotes growth from side shoots, making them much bushier. Growers in commercial nurseries prune conifers annually so as to make the plants bushier and more attractive to the customers.

This subject is, in fact, the one I always get asked about most when I meet would-be conifer gardeners—who are naturally reluctant to take the secateurs to their cherished plants. Consequently, I do not apologise for some repetition on the subject which is also covered to some extent on pages 34 and 35.

There is not space here to give as many details of pruning individual plants as the subject deserves, but there follow some guidelines for the different types of pruning and trimming which may help to improve the conifers in your garden.

Conifer hedges

The subject of hedges is covered

Removing one of the leaders from *Picea pungens* 'Hoopsii'. Take out the one going off at the widest angle.

in detail on page 24 and it will be obvious that the faster growing the hedge, the more often it will need trimming. Thicker branches may need secateurs, but otherwise, if the hedge is trimmed regularly, shears or motorized hedgecutters will do an adequate job. General principles should be to start trimming the sides when a hedge reaches 1-1.5m (4-5ft) and stop the leading shoots when it has reached the required height. If your hedge is to be 2m (6½ft) or more in height it will be advisable to make it narrower in the top 30-60cm (1-2ft), which is where the most vigorous shoots grow. Trim generally in April or August or both.

Taller conifers

Because of the tremendous range of varieties and types of conifer, it is necessary to break them into two distinct groups: (1) those with feathery, fairly dense foliage, and (2) those with a more open habit. (1) Into this category would come the taller *Chamaecyparis lawsoniana* varieties, some cupressus, *Thuja occidentalis, Thuja plicata*, taxus, tsugas and upright junipers. They can mostly be trimmed with shears and although well formed, bushy plants may never need trimming, others that are somewhat misshapen or open in habit will definitely benefit from a certain amount of shearing.

Semi-prostrate junipers can become large and should be pruned when young. They can be cut back drastically if they do reach the size shown here.

being spreading by nature, they need controlling at times. Some grow very large in time. One of the younger junipers is shown on page 31. When they are young is, of course, the time to make your first cuts. When a plant gets much bigger it sometimes requires more drastic measures as you can see from the photograph on the left. Pruning is best undertaken in April or July and August. Try to make the cut immediately underneath a smaller shoot with leaves on it, because if done this way the cut will not be too evident.

Dwarfer conifers

There are many so-called dwarf conifers that do not exactly keep to their name—particularly some that have been grafted. On some richer, more moist soils and in different climatic conditions, growth on the same variety can differ immensely. If you do not prune, some plants that you had originally intended and expected to remain dwarf may run away from you in time. *Picea pungens* 'Globosa' and some pines are cases in point. The former can be trimmed with secateurs in April or May to keep its globose habit and the pines can either be pruned at the same time or even after the first few inches of growth have been made in late spring. These scars are soon hidden by new needles.

Keeping in shape

The above are only a few examples and many other conifers can be improved by careful pruning. I am not in any way advocating that you prune to make neat pillars or rounded balls of all the conifers in your garden—far from it. Most conifers should not have their character or habit changed. It is far better to work with nature and not totally against it while attempting to create better plants in your garden.

(2) The type of conifer with a more open habit would be the mainly taller pines, spruces and firs. Most of the better selections are propagated by grafting (see page 53, which means that they often grow with an irregular habit, particularly when young. These leading shoots will need training in early years (see the photograph on page 45) but so will the sideshoots. This will make a more shapely, densely branched conifer and channel all the energies of the plant into the leading growth. If two leading growths develop, prune away the least attractive one growing at a wider angle. Use secateurs for this purpose.

Use secateurs (and a sturdy pair of garden-worthy gloves) to trim side branches too, making sure to even up the branches that often grow irregularly. The best time for pruning is April or early May, just before new growth begins. You should make your cut just in front of a bud or pair of buds.

Prostrate and semi-prostrate conifers

This will include many varieties of junipers, some abies, picea, pinus, chamaecyparis, tsuga and taxus. The prostrate forms are extremely useful as ground cover plants or specimens in their own right, but,

Possible problems

Most plants have their enemies and although one thinks of conifers as being generally trouble free, they can be attacked by various pests and diseases.

Pests on conifers

There are several insect pests that attack conifers although some only go for certain types, i.e. the pine shoot moth on pinus, spruce gall on Norway spruce (*Picea abies* and its forms). Those are unlikely to be a problem for most gardeners but red spider mite will probably be encountered by most who have a reasonable selection of dwarf conifers. This minute insect is particularly fond of *Picea abies* and *Picea glauca* 'Albertiana Conica' and its effect, while seldom causing death, can be quite marked. The insect sucks the sap from the shoots, the leaves go brown and eventually drop and the plant looks unsightly.

Two or three seasons could go by without an attack of red spider mite but it is in hot, dry, summer periods that it can be at its most voracious. To control, spray twice within two weeks with a systemic insecticide in early summer. It is preferable to spray in the cool of the evening. If the weather remains dry repeat this programme again on those plants most likely to be affected. Apart from picea, chamaecyparis and juniperus types can be attacked, though probably less often.

Believe it or not, ants can provide quite a problem for conifers and heathers (and other plants too for that matter). Even in a wet summer, ants seem to thrive. They build up nests in the middle of plants and can undermine the root system. In George and Angela Edens' garden they had quite a nest in one or two heathers, and in the dwarf conifer border had made a home in the middle of the *Thuja plicata* 'Rogersii'.

Picea abies 'Little Gem' showing signs of an earlier attack of red spider mite.

Cutting out a reverted shoot from *Chamaecyparis obtusa* 'Nana'.

Pull away some of the soil on top to expose the nest and puff in some ant killing dust, then draw the soil back again. Leave for a week or so and inspect. One or two treatments may be necessary in order to eradicate them.

Reversion on dwarf conifers

Most dwarf conifers arose as sports, witches brooms, or from seed. Many have been found in the wild on high mountains where hundreds of years of alpine environment have produced dwarf and stunted forms or clones. We buy dwarf conifers because they are dwarf—however, even with the dwarfest of types one can get a reverting shoot, i.e. it will start to revert to its parent species, usually a large growing tree. If allowed to grow without checking the *Chamaecyparis obtusa* 'Nana' (left in picture) would, instead of reaching perhaps less than 60cm (2ft) in thirty or forty years, grow to 8-10m (24-30ft). Again, a not very likely occurrence, but one of which to be aware.

What not to do
Though primarily this book has guided you on what you should do in your garden to get the best from your plants, it is perhaps worth drawing your attention to some pitfalls you should avoid.

Do not plant specimen conifers too close
Find out first the approximate rate of growth of the conifers you buy, and unless you are prepared to move them at some stage, space at a distance at which they will not eventually spoil each other.

Beware of allowing your conifers to go bare at the base
If you are planting specimens in grass, be sure to allow at least 30cm (12in) of soil around the outside of foliage of your plant and keep enlarging it as the conifer spreads so that you always have this area clear. Apart from making sure that the mower has a fair chance of avoiding your specimen, it will allow air, light and moisture to be received by the conifer. The *Chamaecyparis lawsoniana* 'Ellwoodii' shown on this page is a good example of

the result of letting grass grow up and around the base of the plant.

Likewise, do not allow other plants—and particularly evergreens —to encroach too closely upon those conifers that have foliage down to the ground. If allowed to grow unchecked, they will cut out the light and air and result in your prize specimen going completely brown at the base. I am afraid that I have been guilty myself of allowing this to happen. Trim these other plants back or even be prepared to remove them if you want to protect your specimen.

As a general rule do not trim or prune conifers back into old wood
Once pruned back beyond where there are any green shoots, few conifers will make new growth, and you could be left with a gap which will be hard to disguise except by careful pruning of surrounding branches. Some exceptions to this rule are sequoia and *Thuja plicata*. Start your pruning early.

Beware of large conifers in small gardens
Unless you are actually building or buying a house in established woodland or forest, beware of planting a fast-growing and

eventually large conifer in a handkerchief sized garden. How many times have you seen a large *Cupressocyparis leylandii* or other conifer blocking out the light from a suburban garden. Because it is only 30-45cm (12-18in) tall when you buy it that does not mean that it is a dwarf conifer.

Know when to say goodbye to a conifer
It is amazing how attached some people get to their plants—even when they are, in fact, quite an eyesore, taking up a lot of space and sometimes in danger of demolishing the house during the next gale force wind. I am, of course, exaggerating a little, but sometimes you have to realize that what you have been accustomed to seeing over the years, as part of the garden, may well be better off as firewood.

If you can't tackle the plant yourself, get the local landscaper in to take it down—he or she may even do it for nothing if you offer in return the timber, roots and all. Be positive about your loss. You will be able to gain much more by having the space available to put one or several more attractive plants in place of the one that has gone.

The blue spruce will need a main stem training for some years and strong competing leaders trimmed in summer.

The base of this *Chamaecyparis lawsoniana* 'Ellwoodii' has been starved of light and moisture.

Ideas from other gardens

We can all learn from seeing other people's ideas put into practice. I have been lucky enough to see gardens in many parts of the world where conifers are grown—New Zealand, Japan, the United States and Canada as well as European countries. There is no scope here to deal with the art of bonsai but it, too, offers a way of using conifers to great effect, although it may take a number of years to achieve this.

Although it is interesting to see the larger gardens, it always fascinates me to see how the average home-owner and gardener copes with his garden—and particularly with using conifers. With careful selection dwarf conifers can fulfil a role in the smallest of gardens, as you can see on the following pages. Alpines and dwarf bulbs associate very well with dwarf conifers, and if required can all be grown in pots or containers and changed around from time to time.

If you are a plant collector and enthusiast, then the type of garden Mr Corley created, and which is illustrated on the opposite page, could be for you. However, if you want a garden of year round interest but without too much labour, some of the other gardens may suit your requirements.

Gardening is an individual thing. Get ideas by all means from whatever source, but then add your own particular stamp or style to them.

An unusual informal use of a variety of conifers in front of a Danish house entrance. The conifers are planted in low beds or surrounded by gravel.

An attractive and effective use of a few plants with contrasting shapes and colours. *Pyracantha* 'Orange Glow' gives a bright splash of colour.

This relatively small garden has a wealth of plant material planted for year round interest.

Interesting use is made of a small raised bed at the foot of a patio planted with alpines and dwarf conifers.

The garden of the late Mr R. S. Corley in Naphill, Buckinghamshire provides constant interest. Mr Corley was a dwarf conifer and alpine enthusiast and kept many of his plants small by growing them in pots for some years.

These junipers were planted on a steep, dry bank and although slow to establish have created year round interest. Total groundcover has prevented weeds from growing and the changes in texture and colour are effective.

Alternatives to heathers

If you can grow heathers, why look for an alternative? No reason at all since heathers give you so much value. But if you cannot obtain them or they will not grow in your climate, perhaps it is worth looking for an alternative that will give you both summer and winter colour.

Conifers on their own, of course, can provide the answer and in nearly every climate there are some that will succeed—and there is generally a wider choice than you may imagine. In Britain there is very little limit to the range: literally hundreds can be grown. In Canada and the United States there will be limits set by winter hardiness in the north and summer temperatures in the south.

Make a selection recommended by a specialist nursery in your area—and don't be too narrow-minded.

It is possible to have a garden with nothing but conifers, but I'm not suggesting that that is necessarily advisable. If you cannot grow heathers, conifers can be interspersed with colourful deciduous shrubs that are in scale with the conifers, including dwarf rhododendrons and azaleas. For spring colour use bulbs, and then dwarf perennials and alpines for the summer: aubrieta, phlox, helianthemum, campanulas, alpine geraniums, sedums, to name but a few. But be sure that

they don't invade the conifers too much.

This scheme will give you the patchwork of colour that will create something of interest as much of the year round as possible. I don't pretend to be an expert on American gardens or gardening conditions, but believe that there is more scope there than many gardeners realize.

Few gardeners in Britain appreciate the term 'shade trees' since in Britain and Northern Europe we get few summers that compare with most North American ones. We are usually only too pleased to be able to see the sun and it is seldom too hot to sit out in it. Few conifers like shade, though some junipers and the taxus will tolerate it, particularly where conditions are not too dry. In this case, of course, there are ground covers and a wide range of perennials that will enjoy the shade.

In the open you can plant some of the conifers, shrubs and perennials that will succeed in your climate. Junipers seem to do well in most climates—in fact, in much of North America they have been used too much and are consequently often held in low esteem.

Plants come and go in fashions, but don't forget that it is the way in which plants are *used* that is important. The photographs on this page show the adaptability of conifers, and also what other plants can be used to create a similar effect to that of heathers.

The moveable garden

The photographs accompanying this section will quickly give you the idea I put to British viewers of BBC's Pebble Mill at One. Peter Seabrook (the well-known horticulturist and presenter of the gardening spot on that programme) and I demonstrated the creation of an instant garden—or part of a garden—or, strictly speaking, a raised bed. The plants were kept in the pots they were grown on in at the nursery and simply plunged in peat and sand, with allowances for reasonable drainage.

The idea has some merits for the very small garden where you want to make the most of the space available and even the town garden where there is a reasonable amount of light. You don't have to use just conifers: a few only can either be planted in their pots or taken out and planted if preferred, and some heathers, alpines, bulbs and dwarf shrubs can be added among the conifers to create whatever effect is desired. If left in the pots, they can be moved relatively easily from time to time.

This may mean that you should keep a few pots and potting soil to hand, and use a cold frame or greenhouse to store the plants that have finished flowering or those that are soon to come out. In your little nursery you can pot on any plants you wish into larger pots, propagate

Thuja orientalis 'Aurea Nana' provides a focal point round which are planted (clockwise) *Berberis thunbergii* 'Atropurpurea Nana', *Cotoneaster congestus*, *Helianthemum* 'Firedragon', and a green prostrate juniper, *J. procumbens* 'Nana'. Not a heather in sight.

young plants and generally make a small raised bed, window box or sunken area, a place of continual interest. One word of warning: plants plunged into soil need a bit more looking after than those planted out and established. Water well in summer and do not allow them to become waterlogged in winter. And, of course, look after those that you have in pots.

The moveable garden. The author and Peter Seabrook discussing, planting or plunging 4–5-year-old conifers in a raised bed at the BBC's Pebble Mill studios in Birmingham, England.

Growing conifers in containers

Conifers lend themselves ideally to pots and containers, for small town gardens, for patios, at door entrances, as a focal point or an ornament for both temporary and permanent use.

Containers are, of course, used almost exclusively inside the home for house plants and there seems no logical reason why containers can't be used more outside. They offer adaptability and mobility (depending, of course, on their size), allowing one to change the garden scene more easily than more permanent plantings.

The advantage of containers is that compost can be obtained to suit almost any type of plant: if, for instance, you wish to grow summer flowering heathers or other acid loving plants, you can choose your soil or compost accordingly.

Who can say that I don't give both sides of an argument? I have to admit that plants in containers will generally need much more looking after than if their root system was allowed to run free in the soil. They will also need feeding regularly. I am sure we have all seen conifers and other evergreens, displayed in tubs or containers, that have all but given up the ghost. Conifers do need regular watering, particularly in the summer and maintained in good health with either a regular liquid feed or a slow release fertilizer, both of which can be obtained in garden centres.

Hardiness

Plants in containers will suffer more from extremes of heat and cold than those in the open ground. During periods of severe freezing temperatures, roots may freeze: a danger for evergreens in particular since they will be unable to draw any moisture into their system to support the foliage, and desiccation and death may be the result. Conifers don't generally tend to show their distress until it is too late, well after the damage to the roots has occurred and the plant needs to start growing again. However, in most parts of Britain severe winters are not likely to cause too much damage to conifers that are in a large enough container and have a well-established root system before the winter. A thorough spraying with an anti-desiccant spray would nonetheless be a worthwhile investment in early December, or earlier, depending upon your locality.

Types of container

The choice of containers is a wide one, and with container and patio gardening now so popular, ever widening. Stone must be the most classical, but whether natural or reconstituted, it will be expensive. There is likely to be less fluctuation in temperature and more protection from frost in stone than in either clay pottery or artificial materials. Treated timber—rounded logs or wine or beer barrels or sleepers—can also make attractive raised beds or containers.

There are some reasonable plastic containers available and although they are hardly a convincing imitation, they do have the advantage of less weight, more retention of water in summer, and last but not least, relative cheapness.

Planting

The sequence of planting containers is illustrated on this page. There are a few basic rules to follow: the first being to ensure that you have adequate drainage.

Place some moist compost in the tub, enough to bring the top of the plant's rootball just below the rim. Remove the nursery container.

Put the plant into the tub so that the base of the foliage is just above soil level, which should be about 3cm (1¼in) below the rim of the tub.

Firm lightly and water thoroughly all round the plant two or three times to make sure the compost is fully soaked. Water regularly and feed.

Often you may buy containers with no drainage holes at the base. Depending on the type of container, you will need to make sure that there are reasonable sized holes at the base. In a lightweight container it will also be advisable to use some ballast in the form of broken stone or 3-cm (1-in) diameter gravel or shingle—which will also assist drainage in winter. Put between 5-10cm (2-4in) of this material at the base.

Composts

You can obtain a proprietary compost for most container plants from garden centres or mix your own. Around 10 per cent loam 60 per cent peat and 30 per cent grit would be reasonable with added fertilizer. Mix thoroughly and if possible use sterilized, weed-free loam.

Follow general rules as for open ground planting but remember, too, that for a temporary planting—say, if you only want conifers in your container in the winter—you can keep the plant in its nursery container and remove it late in the spring if required. When plants begin to get too big or crowd each other, you may need to plant them in the garden or put them in a larger container.

Above Juniperus horizontalis 'Hughes' to the right of the door. *Picea pungens* 'Hoopsii' on the left of the door.

Below This stone sink has been planted up with a variety of alpine plants and miniature forms of dwarf conifers.

Effectively grouped in containers are Juniperus scopulorum 'Skyrocket', *J. horizontalis* 'Hughes' and *J.* x *media* 'Old Gold'. See pages 60 and 61.

The start of it all

The popular image of a nursery as a small unit with a few people pottering about producing plants by old and timeworn methods is one which is seldom near reality. That there *are* such nurseries still in existence is probably true, but most would have gone out of business years ago.

Today most large nurseries are modern, efficient production units and to some extent somewhat akin to the factory. This may be regrettable in some ways, but pure economics have pushed the less efficient out of business. There is, thank goodness, still room for the smaller specialists and they serve an extremely useful purpose within the industry.

To run a nursery business these days requires forward planning, highly-trained staff, and management and feet firmly placed on the ground. With some crops taking five years or more before they are able to be sold, careful decisions have to be made a long way ahead.

Not only are general business principles of importance, but knowledge of a great many other aspects will be necessary in running a successful nursery. Such things as the plants themselves and their individual requirements, chemicals for sterilization, for pest and weed control, irrigation and electronics, general machinery and a host of more detailed and specific data will be required. It is an international business, as can be seen from some of the photographs shown on these pages.

When young cuttings have been rooted they must be

A propagation bench on a New Zealand nursery. This is a skilled job.

The inside of a modern propagation house with controlled conditions.

Lines of young conifer plants ready for sale or potting on.

Specimen conifers in large containers growing on in preparation for sale.

hardened off and then potted. Most nurseries use machines for this operation. They will be potted first into a small pot and then either sold at that stage as a young plant or potted on into larger pots or containers. This process can be repeated for a number of years with plants being sold at certain ages or sizes.

Conifers, like all plants, will need watering and feeding to keep them growing and healthy. They must be spaced widely enough in the beds so that they fill out and don't become thin or bare at the base. This must happen at each stage of a plant's development. Some conifers, such as *Picea pungens* cultivars and other upright grafted forms, will need the main shoot training with a cane and side branches trimmed to make a good shape.

Care and attention is needed at all stages if a quality plant is to be finally produced.

When the plants reach a saleable size then they will be offered for sale to garden centres or other nurseries and delivered in a fresh condition. The garden centre will display them and offer them for sale to the general gardening public—and will be responsible for making sure that those plants are maintained in top condition for sale. At times, this can be difficult unless proper facilities exist for watering and feeding. Some nurseries and some garden centres fall short of the ideal, but in the end it is up to the gardener to ask and be sure not to expect less than top quality. Generally, the adage that you get what you pay for holds true in horticulture.

Trimming the base of the cutting or scion.

Preparing the understock. Make an identical cut to fit the scion.

Fit the scion to the understock matching the cut surfaces.

Bind the scion and understock together with grafting tape.

easy and others difficult to root.

Basically a side shoot with a heel attached is used from an older plant, trimmed lightly and placed upright in a medium of peat and sand. For easy-rooting subjects a cold frame or cloche can be used successfully, but a rather more professional and quicker method is a glasshouse with bottom heat and possibly automatic mist to keep cuttings from drying out. The more sophisticated the system the more easily it can go wrong. Hormone rooting dips or powders give an added benefit when difficult subjects are being rooted. Some conifers may root within four weeks, others may take more than six months, and some may not root at all!

Grafting

This method is used where it has proved either uneconomical or impossible to root conifers from cuttings. It is a very skilled job indeed, comprising not only the slower work of the grafting process, but the careful attention required nursing the new grafts through the incubating period before stock and scion become a successful union. The stock refers to the understock or rootstock —or simply a compatible seedling of about two years old and potted. The scion is the cutting from the desired plant. The stock for *Picea pungens* cultivars, for instance, would be two to three-year seedlings of *Picea abies*. The photographs show how the grafting process is carried out. Many of the abies, piceas and most of the pinus cultivars must be propagated by grafting, making them naturally an expensive item to produce and consequently to buy. The average number of saleable plants which arises from a batch of one hundred grafts of *Picea pungens* 'Kosteri' on most nurseries is only sixty—and this is the result of work by skilled nurserymen.

Propagation

Many conifers can be propagated from seed and this is how the forestry industry produces the millions of young trees it needs for eventual timber production. This would include such common types as the Scots pine *Pinus sylvestris,* and the Norway spruce *Picea abies.* There are almost no named cultivars, however, of any conifer that will come true from seed and these have to be increased by cuttings or grafting.

Cuttings

This is a relatively straightforward method, but among the range of conifers that can be produced from cuttings, some will be very

Selecting conifers

Let's assume you have decided on planting some conifers in your garden. Where do you go to find the plants you require? And how can you tell whether you are getting good quality plants?

Garden centres

There are large and small garden centres, good and bad. Although it is probably true to say that you will not find as large a range of conifers on a garden centre as you might on a specialist nursery, many garden centres stock a wide choice.

You have the advantage of selecting your own plants, it is to be hoped in the sizes required. All conifers and other plants should be clearly labelled and advice should be available, although some garden centres may fall short on some of these points. It is important that plants are labelled with the correct name, with some estimate given as to its probable rate of growth.

You will find most plants offered for sale at a garden centre are pot or container grown. Although conifers are, and can be, safely sold and transplanted with a rootball wrapped in hessian sacking, they will need rather more aftercare to establish than container plants.

Specialist nurseries

There are a few nurseries which specialise in conifers or dwarf conifers and these are usually despatched by mail order. The advantage of going to a specialist is that a wider choice is available and you can almost be certain that plants are true to name. The disadvantages being that generally only relatively small sizes of plants

The specimen of *Thuja occidentalis* 'Rheingold' is about fourteen years old. Plants from two to six years are shown in front.

A twenty-year-old specimen of *Thuja orientalis* 'Aurea Nana' in the background with plants from one to six years old in front.

can be sent by post or road and that you cannot see the plants before you buy them. So the choice is yours.

Quality

A difficult matter to establish without seeing the plants, but generally they should look healthy and fresh, not starved or stunted. They should have foliage more or less to the base of the plant, and not have bare or brown patches. They should, in practically all cases, be of good shape (although some forms are naturally irregular in habit).

I have seen conifers at garden centres which are an absolute disgrace and should never be offered for sale. With many types of plants, poor quality can be outgrown after a year or two in the garden, but conifers such as the *Chamaecyparis lawsoniana* varieties, which are often sold bare at the base, will seldom outgrow those bare patches which will remain an eyesore for many years.

Value for money

The point that really needs to be made is that you should be aware of *what* you are buying. Here I am mainly referring to sizes and ages of conifers and relative cost. Time to a nurseryman is usually measured in years and these are broken down into seasons. Compare, for instance, a *Chamaecyparis lawsoniana* 'Columnaris' with a *Chamaecyparis lawsoniana* 'Gnome'. At the age of ten years the former can be expected to be a specimen 2.5m (approx. 8ft) in height, whilst the latter may be only 30cm (1ft) high by as much wide. Because of its size and weight and the cost of handling, carriage etc., the *C.l.* 'Columnaris' will be much more expensive than the *C.l.* 'Gnome' —although to the average gardener the smaller plant may still seem expensive in comparison. But *any* plant that has had to be looked after and grown by a nurseryman for ten years should be realistically priced.

I have always attempted to get across the point of relative sizes and ages of conifers, and I think that the pictures on this page give a good indication of how important a factor this is when selecting plants for your garden.

Making the choice

The selection of conifers that follows is only a sample of some of the best dwarf conifers available, but is intended to give an idea of the variety of types that you can consider using in your garden. Some, but not all, of these are included in the plan for Mr and Mrs Edens' garden.

The point has already been emphasized about the importance of selecting conifers for their interest and habit but above all growth rates. The fact that there are now conifers available for practically every size of garden—and nearly every soil and situation—gives you a very wide choice. A visit to gardens where there is a good selection of conifers will give you more perspective than studying catalogues and books, although this, too, can be helpful. Many garden centres that stock a good range may have a resident expert to whom you can go for advice.

I have made for each conifer described an estimate of probable rates of growth after ten years: this is necessarily approximate because of the wide range of climatic and cultural conditions which exist in different countries and areas. The letter H denotes probable height and S probable spread.

Abies, the Silver Firs

There are some first class dwarf forms of the abies, most of which have to be propagated by grafting, whereas the taller growing forest trees are grown from seed. Most will grow in reasonable garden soil given adequate moisture but some will struggle on thin chalk soils. Generally they are very hardy but new shoots can be susceptible to spring frosts.

Abies balsamea 'Hudsonia'

A compact, slow growing shrub of rounded habit with dark green upper leaves and like many firs, silver beneath. Brown winter buds

Abies procera 'Glauca Prostrata'.

form through the winter to swell and burst into bright green new growth in late spring. A reliable dwarf. H 30cm (12in) × S 50cm (20in).

Abies concolor 'Compacta'

Worth looking for is this dwarf form of the Colorado white fir with deepish blue grey, widely spaced leaves and a somewhat open branching habit, becoming denser with age. Some pruning may help create a bushier habit. The blue intensifies during and after new growth in early

summer. This form is grafted. H 60-90cm (24-36in) × S 60-75cm (24-30in).

Abies koreana

The Korean fir is a worthwhile garden conifer, making a slow start in life but eventually forming a tree of some 15m (50ft) or more. But don't be put off by that because it will probably take at least ten years to reach 3m (10ft) and probably well before that time will have amazed you with its startling purple blue cones. These stand above the branches, clothed in rich green leaves which are bright silver beneath. It makes a narrow pyramid, well worth a place with other ornamental conifers and not difficult to grow. H 1.80m-2.40m (6-8ft).

There is a slower growing and somewhat rare form with light, butter yellow leaves *Abies koreana* 'Aurea', but this will be scarce and more expensive because it is grafted and slightly more difficult to grow.

Abies lasiocarpa 'Compacta'
(also known as *Abies arizonica* 'Glauca Compacta')
This superb conifer is one of my favourites. A dwarf for many years, it makes a broad pyramid of silvery blue foliage. Attractive brown winter buds erupt in late spring into intense silver blue shoots. A grafted form. H 60-90cm (24-36in) × S 60-90cm (24-36in) at base.

Abies procera 'Glauca Prostrata' (also known as *Abies nobilis* 'Glauca Prostrata')
A selected form of the large growing noble fir this has an irregular, spreading form. At its best makes a carpet of blue grey needles or leaves and bright blue spring shoots. Occasional upright growths should be cut out. A beautiful specimen when grown against contrasting foliage plants. Not suitable for shallow chalk soils. A grafted form. H 30-40cm (12-16in) × S 60-90cm (24-36in).

Abies nordmanniana 'Golden Spreader'
For those who like winter colour, this form of the Caucasian fir is ideal, for its best colour comes in the shorter days of the year. Initially prostrate with golden yellow leaves, a leading shoot may form to make an irregular upright bush. Cut out if you want it to remain prostrate. In full sun might be prone to scorch in warmer climates. Grafted. H 20-30cm (8-12in) × S 30-50cm (12-18in).

Abies lasiocarpa 'Compacta'.

Abies nordmanniana 'Golden Spreader'.

Cedrus, the Cedars

The cedars are a small family of distinct appearance and whilst the majority will eventually make large trees, there are some interesting and attractive dwarf forms for garden use.

Generally hardy throughout the British Isles, but not reliably so in more northerly or extreme climates—as one might expect of species which originate in areas around the Mediterranean and in the lower Himalayan range. Generally preferring a well drained, loamy soil, they will succeed on heavy clay soils where not too wet. Forms of *Cedrus atlantica* and *Cedrus libani* are hardier and will accept much drier conditions than *C. deodara* and its varieties.

Cedrus atlantica 'Glauca'

The blue cedar or atlas cedar is one of the most striking of all conifers but it does need space to develop. Fast growing and wide spreading, it is not a plant to recommend for an average suburban garden, since it will eventually make a tree more than 35m (100ft) high. I have seen plants that have been trimmed from an early age to form a pillar one metre (3ft) or so wide—a possible alternative worth considering. It has bright silver-blue leaves or needles the year round on stiff branches that extend upwards from the main stem. It will require its leading shoot to be trained upwards from an early age, with a cane—but by the time that leader reaches 2-3m (6-10ft), it will be away. H 3-4m (10-13ft) × S 2-3m (6-10ft).

There is a golden leaved form *C.a.* 'Aurea' which I have found a poor grower, prone to scorch, and would not recommend. More spectacular, though hardly generally available, is the amazing *Cedrus atlantica* 'Glauca Pendula' which untrained would run about on the ground but carefully trained by the nurseryman makes an arch, or weeping tree,

Cedrus deodara 'Golden Horizon'.

following any direction you want it to take. All are grafted.

Cedrus deodara 'Golden Horizon'

A form of the deodar cedar which comes in variable shapes and sizes. It can be prostrate and this is one of the most attractive and recognizable forms, but it can also make a leading shoot or shoots—in which case you might, without pruning, end up with a semi-prostrate or upright form. It has golden yellow leaves, maintained the year round but brighter during the summer months after new growth has emerged. It could be expected to grow 60-75cm (24-30in) in height with a spread of 90-120cm (36-48in) or more.

A golden leaved form which I think highly of is the very graceful *Cedrus deodara* 'Nana Aurea' with soft golden yellow foliage. It takes some time to make a dense, well-formed plant but as a specimen takes some beating with its graceful, pendulous, tipped branches. H 1.50-2.40m (5-8ft). Other golden leaved, upright forms, such as *C.d.* 'Gold Mound' and *C.d.* 'Gold Cone' promise to give us more selection in this range of attractive conifers, which make ideal specimens in a lawn.

Cedrus libani 'Sargentii'

A first class conifer for the smaller garden, this will be worth looking for, since it is without doubt still fairly rare, though originally introduced in the 1920s. It is slow growing and though, without training, will initially be prostrate in habit, gradually builds up into a rounded dome of drooping branches clothed in light green leaves. It makes a perfect specimen planted on a slope or at the top of a wall from where it can cascade. Alternatively, it can be trained up to 60-90cm (24-36in) or more to form a graceful, pendulous bush of some character. In ten years, without training, expect it to be 30-40 cm (12-16in) in height with a spread of 60-90cm (24-36in).

Chamaecyparis, the False Cypress

Although not native to Europe, this family, with its ancestors in North America and the Orient is among the most widely used and planted of garden conifers. Its popularity exists because of the wide range of shapes, sizes and colours available for garden use. Most species and cultivars prefer adequate moisture and good drainage, but dislike exposed positions and cold drying winds.

Chamaecyparis lawsoniana 'Gimbornii'

One of the most attractive dwarf conifers forming a perfect dome-shaped bush in time. The foliage is blue-green and soft to the touch.
H 60cm (24in) × S 50cm (20in).

Chamaecyparis lawsoniana 'Minima Aurea'

Without doubt one of the best of all dwarf conifers. Very slow-growing, compact branching system and beautiful, golden yellow foliage the year round. Forms a tight pyramid after many years.
H 30-40cm (12-16in) × S 30cm (12in).

Chamaecyparis obtusa 'Nana Gracilis'

A dwarf form of the Hinoki cypress of Japan, this has been a favourite conifer for many years. Large, glossy green, shell-shaped foliage sprays. Often sold as a grafted plant which is generally quicker growing than those propagated by cuttings.
H 50-60cm (20-24in) × S 50-60cm (20-24in).

Chamaecyparis obtusa 'Nana Lutea'

One of my favourite dwarf conifers, this beautiful golden leaved form of the Hinoki cypress is a real gem. Very slow growing in early years, it gradually forms an irregular bush of dense habit and somewhat twisted 'whorls' of light golden yellow foliage. In full sun it will be brighter in appearance and may occasionally

Chamaecyparis lawsoniana 'Pembury Blue'.

scorch, but given some protection from exposed positions will maintain a deeper golden yellow—and in deep shade will hardly look yellow at all. H 45-60cm (18-24in) × 30-45cm (12-18in). This variety is far superior to the somewhat looser growing and less golden form known as C.o. 'Nana Aurea'.

Chamaecyparis pisifera 'Filifera Aurea'

As for many conifers, a cumbersome name for a most distinct and attractive plant. Known as the golden mop cypress, it has rather lax, thread-like foliage which gradually builds up to form a broad bush of bright golden yellow. It can be trimmed at the sides as it develops to make a more formal shape. Excellent for winter colour where it associates well with winter flowering heathers. H 60-90cm (24-36in) × S 60-90cm (24-36in). There is a green foliage form of more compact habit C.p. 'Filifera Nana' and one with variegated foliage appropriately called C.p. 'Filifera Aureovariegata', both of

Chamaecyparis pisifera 'Filifera Aurea'.

C.l. 'Columnaris', an attractive plant with a narrow, columnar habit, while more open but of an intense silver blue colour is *C.l.* 'Pembury Blue', improved by the occasional trim. There are a great many forms with golden leaves: *C.l.* 'Dutch Gold' seems to keep a good colour most of the year and is naturally dense in habit; *C.l.* 'Lanei' maintains the brightest golden yellow in winter but needs space outwards as well as upwards to develop and, lastly, *C.l.* 'Stardust' has a nice name and makes an attractive broad column in time. Blues and yellows need to be set off by more sober greens and in my opinion the narrow form and rich green foliage of *C.l.* 'Green Pillar' takes some beating. *C.l.* 'Green Hedger' is of a similar colour but much broader in outline and excellent for hedges.

Most of the above can be expected to grow 2-3m (6-10ft) in ten years and may ultimately make quite tall trees. If you want to make beautiful specimens, remember to keep grass, weeds and other plants well clear of the base as your lawsons develop.

Chamaecyparis lawsoniana 'Ellwoodii'

This is almost too common to need description, being Britain's most popular conifer. Dwarf it is not, although often described as such, making a broad column of dark blue green, densely packed foliage, perhaps 1.8-2m (6-7ft) in ten years but ultimately 8-10m (24-30ft). For a dwarf replica of *C.l.* 'Ellwoodii' I recommend *C.l.* 'Ellwood's Pillar'. This is much more compact and slower growing with feathery, blue grey foliage and in ten years reaches less than 1m (3ft). One other form which arose from *C.l.* 'Ellwoodii' as a sport or different coloured shoot is *C.l.* 'Ellwood's Gold' with soft yellow green foliage, brighter in summer than winter.

which become more attractive as they mature.

Some taller varieties

It is difficult to select just one of the many forms of upright lawsons available. Better to give you a recommended selection from the great many that are in cultivation. As a general rule, those described briefly below will grow on most soils where reasonable moisture yet adequate drainage exists. They could be classed as medium growers, which go to create a backcloth to the lawn or garden but do need space to develop their best form. They can be interspersed with other medium or taller-growing conifers to create a change in colour and texture—the blue spruces, for instance, make ideal companions. Reliably hardy in Britain, they will not grow well in more severe climates, although, being native to the West coast of North America, they are hardier than one might imagine. For blues look for the popular form

Juniperus scopulorum 'Blue Heaven'.

Juniperus, the Junipers

The junipers are some of the most versatile and useful of garden conifers. They are generally tough and hardy and will grow on most soils, including those containing lime. They usually prefer sun and reasonable drainage. Of the great number of varieties in cultivation, regrettably few can be mentioned.

Juniperus communis 'Compressa'

A real miniature with a perfect cone shape. It has tightly adpressed foliage with leaves of grey-green which are an attractive silver beneath. Although accepted as hardy it can 'burn' from cold easterly winds in exposed situations. Ideal for the small garden or rock garden.
H 30-45cm (12-18in).

Juniperus horizontalis 'Hughes'

One of the most attractive of the carpet junipers and an excellent form used as ground cover. Neat spreading habit, blue-grey in winter turning a shining silver-grey in summer. An easy plant.
H 20-30cm (8-12in) × S 1.2-1.5m (4-5ft).

There are many more prostrate conifers. The flattest growing are *Juniperus horizontalis* 'Glauca' and, almost indistinguishable from it, *J.h.* 'Wiltonii'. These form a carpet of blue, made more dense if the long growths are trimmed occasionally. Slightly higher off the ground is one of the best forms, *J.h.* 'Blue Chip', its feathery foliage a most intense silver blue, particularly in summer.

Juniperus x media 'Mint Julep'

An introduction with a rather American sounding name—not surprising since it has recently been introduced to Europe from the United States. Semi-prostrate form with arching branches and foliage, a rich green the year through. Ideal for use as an accent plant and in contrast to golden forms. Can be trimmed to form an attractive low hedge.
H 75-90cm (30-36in) × S 1.2-1.5m (4-5ft).

Juniperus x media 'Old Gold'

One of my favourites, and without doubt one of the best of the semi-prostrate junipers. Dense spreading habit which, unlike the more vigorous *Juniperus* x *media* 'Pfitzerana Aurea', needs little trimming. More golden than the latter with new growth in spring, particularly attractive. Needs to be planted in full sun for best colour (as do all golden forms). A good corner or accent plant and when established not an easy bush to damage.
H 1-1.2m (3-4ft) × S 1.25-1.5m (4-5ft).

Of the many similar golden foliaged semi-prostrate varieties of *Juniperus* x *media* I would recommend in particular *J.* x *m.* 'Gold Coast'. This is generally lower growing and maintains a brighter colour the year through—even brighter than 'Old Gold' itself.

Juniperus scopulorum 'Skyrocket'

Perhaps the narrowest form of the Rocky Mountain juniper in general cultivation and certainly aptly named. An easy, trouble free plant and excellent where an upright accent is needed, such as among heathers or prostrate conifers. Older specimens can be liable to open up if heavy snow occurs, but otherwise the narrow form is not likely to exceed 30cm (12in) in width. Approximate height in ten years 1.85-2.4m (6-8ft). 'Skyrocket' was one of the first and most popular upright varieties but there are many others. Similar, slower growing and more dense in habit is *J.s.* 'Gray Gleam', the name aptly describing the foliage. Broader and quite vigorous is *J.s.* 'Blue Heaven', silver blue and probably improved by an occasional trim.

Juniperus squamata 'Blue Carpet'

This conifer of recent introduction is a most distinctive form, useful as a single specimen and also for ground cover planting. It has a low-growing, spreading habit with branches slightly upturned and 'nodding' at the tips. The foliage is an intense silver blue in summer, dulling slightly in winter. It can be pruned to improve density or to restrict growth.
H 20-30cm (8-12in) × S 1.5-2m (5-6ft).

There are two other first class forms of *Juniperus squamata* worth mentioning. First the variety *J.s.* 'Holger', which has a similar habit to 'Blue Carpet' but with creamy yellow shoots in early summer spreading to the whole plant but toning down in winter. One of the best of all junipers is *J.s.* 'Blue Star', a compact but irregular bush of steel blue foliage. It looks good as a small plant and as a mature one, in ten years.
H 30-40cm (12-16in) × S 40-50cm (16-20in).

Juniperus procumbens 'Nana'

This is a most attractive juniper with a really prostrate creeping habit, ideal for banks or for overhanging walls. It has fresh apple green foliage, quite prickly to the touch, which makes a dense carpet and although slow in growth to begin with eventually has a wide spread.
H 10-15cm (4-6in) × S 1.5-1.85m (5-6ft).

Juniperus horizontalis 'Hughes'.

Juniperus x *media* 'Gold Coast'.

Picea orientalis 'Aurea'.

Picea pungens 'Globosa'.

Picea, the Spruces

One of the largest family or genus of conifer with a range including both forest trees and dwarfs of many shapes and sizes. The spruces are adaptable to most soils but do not succeed so well where it is too dry and chalky. Most are best planted in a reasonably open position. New shoots can be susceptible to spring frosts and some are prone to attack by red spider mite and other pests (see page 44).

Picea abies 'Little Gem'

A really compact dwarf form of the Norway spruce, 'Little Gem' is aptly named for its year round attractive appearance. It is particularly striking when new, fresh green shoots appear in early summer. Ideal for the rock garden.

H 20-30cm (8-12in) × S 20-30cm (8-12in).

Picea pungens 'Globosa'

Until recently this has been almost a collector's item due to its scarcity, but now should be freely available in Britain. It is a very beautiful dwarf form of the blue spruce which need not be an embarrassment even in the smallest garden. Dense, bushy, irregularly rounded habit with intense, silver blue needles, it is particularly striking in early summer. Brown winter buds. Most plants will be grafted.

H 45-60cm (18-24in) × S 60-70cm (24-28in).

Picea glauca 'Albertiana 'Conica'

This is perhaps the best-known and most popular dwarf spruce of all, and makes a green pyramid of almost perfect symmetry. Winter buds form to be broken when bright, fresh, green shoots appear in late spring. These can be susceptible to spring frosts and the plant to attack from red spider mite, although this can be controlled.

H 100–125cm (40–50in).

Several dwarfer forms exist and make distinctive garden plants. *P.g.* 'Alberta Globe' is as one might imagine, a much more rounded form, reaching only 45-60cm (18-24in) in ten years by as much in width. The dwarfest of all and still quite rare is *P.g.* 'Laurin', a really miniature 'Alberta Spruce' with short, dark green needles.

H 30cm (12in) only in ten years.

Picea pungens 'Hoopsii'

There are many selected forms of the *Picea pungens glauca*, the Colorado blue spruce, which can only be propagated by grafting, and there are many arguments over which is the best. In the end it can only be a matter of personal opinion. However (in my opinion) 'Hoopsii' would certainly be a contender as one of the best. Perhaps it takes time to make a good shape, but it is without doubt one of the bluest forms, with quite long, bright, silver-blue leaves. A medium grower which, like other upright growing forms, needs the leader training for some years with a cane (see page 45). It may need some pruning in early years to make a regular form.

Other notable varieties with a similar rate of growth are *P.p.* 'Koster', *P.p.* 'Hoto' and *P.p.* 'Moerheimii'.
H 1-2.5m (3-8ft).

Picea orientalis 'Aurea'
(syn. *Picea orientalis* 'Aureospicata). This can eventually make quite a large tree, although slow growing in its early years. It has tightly adpressed, dark green needles and for much of the year has quite an unremarkable appearance. But when new shoots appear in May or early June they are a beautiful golden yellow colour and the tree then stands out like a beacon among its surroundings. Through the summer the yellow shoots gradually tone down, so that by late autumn the tree returns to its former guise. To achieve this unusual transformation it should be planted in full sun.
H 2-3m (6-9ft).

Picea omorika 'Nana'
This is an attractive dwarf form of the Serbian spruce, notable for its extremely compact, pyramidal habit and silver-blue, stomatic bands beneath the leaves. These are a prominent feature against the mid-green of the rest as can be seen from the accompanying photograph. Very slow growing in its early years it will eventually form a specimen reaching some 5-6m (16-18ft). An easy-growing conifer with few faults.
H 60-75cm (24-30in) × S 60-75cm (24-30in).

Picea abies 'Little Gem'.

Picea glauca 'Albertiana Conica'.

Pinus, the Pines

It is only possible here to show and describe a few in the very wide range of species, varieties and cultivars of pines many of which are excellent garden plants. Until recently they were little known and dwarf forms were difficult to obtain. Now the situation has changed and the gardener has a much wider choice readily available.

They are different from most other conifers in having needle-like foliage in bundles from two to five. Many, including some dwarf forms, produce their cones quite freely, which is an added attraction.

Pines generally dislike a polluted or industrial atmosphere, and too much shade. Many will grow in poor, impoverished conditions but others dislike shallow chalk soils. Nearly all dwarf forms must be propagated by grafting.

Pinus leucodermis 'Compact Gem'

This slow growing conifer may not look too spectacular as a small grafted plant but it soon begins to form a rounded bush of dark green, creating considerable appeal. When associated with golden foliage heathers or other contrasting plants around its base, it becomes even more striking —definitely to be recommended, although in time it will outgrow the small garden.
Growing to H 120-150cm (4-5ft) × S 80-100cm (30-40in) in ten years.

On the other hand P.l. 'Schmidtii' would not be likely to outgrow any garden, being one of the most miniature pines in existence, and a treasure to any collector or enthusiast. It makes a rounded ball of prickly, dark green needles and in ten years can only be expected to grow H 30cm × S 30cm (12 × 12in). If you are lucky enough to obtain a specimen be sure to give it good drainage.

Pinus leucodermis 'Compact Gem'.

Pinus parviflora 'Glauca'

A selection of the Japanese white pine with beautiful light blue needles in clusters of five. Its slightly-leaning outline and irregular branching habit are typical of what one might imagine in a Japanese garden. Blue green cones at an early age give it an added attraction.
H 1.8-2.5m (6-8ft).

Similar though faster growing is P.p. 'Templehof', and slower but more dense in habit the attractive P.p. 'Negishii'. All the parviflora species require good drainage.

Pinus densiflora 'Umbraculifera'

This dwarf form of the Japanese white pine, P. densiflora, has two of its own picturesque names, the Tanyosho or umbrella pine. It was given the latter for its upright, spreading, branching system which becomes more pronounced as the plant matures. Densely packed, dark green leaves and attractive new shoots in spring.
H 75-120cm (2½-4ft) × S 90-120cm (3-4ft).

Pinus mugo 'Mops'

Perhaps the most reliable dwarf form of Pinus mugo, the

Pinus mugo 'Mops'.

mountain pine, 'Mops' has a distinctive name and a distinctive rounded, low growing form, deal for the rock garden. It has tightly held grey-green needles and attractive winter buds.
H 30-40cm (12-16in) × S 50-60cm (20-24in).

Three other distinct *P. mugo* forms are worth mentioning; first the compact, rounded *P.m.* 'Humpy', aptly named and ideal for the rock garden; also green but prostrate and spreading in habit is *P.m.* 'Corley's Mat', perfect for banks or hanging over walls; and lastly the very striking *P.m.* 'Ophir' which has dark green needles in summer, changing in winter to bright golden yellow in full sun. Similar to *P.m.* 'Mops' in habit.

Pinus strobus 'Nana'
A dwarf, five needled form of the white pine and a most attractive garden conifer. It has long, bluish-green needles soft to the touch and a compact bushy habit wider than high. The foliage remains completely clothed to the base of the plant for a great many years. There are one or two other forms of similar habit.
H 50-75cm (20-30in) × S 80-100cm (31-39in).

Pinus sylvestris 'Fastigiata'
There are many distinct forms of the Scots pine, Britain's only native pine, but this is perhaps the most striking for its narrow fastigiate form although it is by no means a dwarf. Blue grey needles and upright branching give it a character of its own. Useful, too, in the smaller garden because of its lack of width.
H 250-300cm (8-10ft) × S 45-60cm (18-24in).

There are few plants which truly give a long period of winter colour, and the golden forms of *Pinus sylvestris* are outstanding value for this purpose. *P.s.* 'Aurea' comes in one or two clones or forms: one with light yellow leaves and more open habit, the other slower growing and more compact, particularly in its early years, with deep golden-yellow foliage.
H 180-250cm (5-8ft) × S 120-150cm (4-5ft).

More compact is *P.s.* 'Gold Coin' probably similar, I believe, to the form just described, since it has the same colour, and without trimming soon develops a leading shoot which, if left, would eventually make a plant of tree like proportions. For all that, still worth having—although remember that these forms have golden needles only in winter, changing to green in summer.

Pinus sylvestris 'Aurea'.

Taxus, the Yews

The yews are used little in gardens in Britain these days yet are some of the most useful and adaptable plants. Not all are of sombre, 'churchyard' appearance. They grow well on chalk and the green forms succeed in shade where few other conifers will grow. Many are excellent for hedges and withstand clipping well but all dislike poor drainage. In North America the hardier forms of *Taxus cuspidata*, the Japanese yew, and *Juniperus* x *media* are used for landscape, as they are tougher plants, if less exciting than *Taxus baccata*, the English yew.

Taxus baccata 'Standishii'

This form of the Irish yew is a choice plant and extremely slow growing, though not difficult. It has a narrow, fastigiate outline when established and rich old-gold foliage, particularly pronounced when making new growth in early summer. Not to be confused with the faster growing and less golden *Taxus baccata* 'Fastigiata Aurea'. 'Standishii' is an equally attractive plant during both winter and summer.
H 90-120cm (3-4ft).

Taxus baccata 'Summergold'

This introduction is most useful as a specimen and a ground cover plant. It has a wide, spreading, semi-prostrate habit which is perhaps a little open on young plants. A little pruning will soon make a denser bush. Yellow-green foliage in winter turns a bright summer gold, hence, no doubt, the name. Easy and trouble free but needs to be grown in a position in full sun for best colour.
H 40-50cm (16-20in) × S 1-1.4m (3-4½ft).

Taxus baccata 'Repandens'

Low growing and eventually wide spreading this has dark, shiny, almost black green foliage but is a most useful plant for ground cover, particularly in dry, shady situations. It will, of course, grow equally well in full sun. If there is a tendency for the prostrate branches to become irregular in habit then trimming them back will result in a denser and more attractive bush.
H 45cm (18in) × S 90-150cm (3-5ft).

Taxus baccata 'Semperaurea'.

Thuja, the Arbor-vitaes

A great many useful and attractive garden conifers have arisen from the three thuja species: *Thuja occidentalis*, the white cedar or American arbor-vitae, *Thuja orientalis*, the Chinese arbor-vitae, and *Thuja plicata*, the western red cedar. All have similar flattened branchlets and scale like overlapping leaves; some have a pungent or aromatic foliage—the choice of term according to one's taste.

Thujas can be grown in most soils but dislike poor drainage or swampy conditions. The hardiest is *Thuja occidentalis*, followed by *T. plicata* and *T. orientalis* but all would be considered hardy in Britain.

Thuja occidentalis 'Danica'

There are few conifers possessing the rich green of this Danish introduction, although it does become somewhat bronze tinged in winter. A dwarf form of rounded globular habit and vertically held, flattened foliage sprays, it is, I think, the best of the many and often confusingly named dwarf green *Thuja occidentalis* cultivars.
H 30-45cm (12-18in) × S 50-60cm (20-24in).

However, it is worth mentioning one or two other dwarf forms since they are generally quite tough and hardy. One of the most compact is *T.o.* 'Hetz Midget', making a globular bush of dark green foliage.
H 30cm × S 30cm (12 × 12in) in ten years.

Slightly more dense and distinctive is *T.o.* 'Recurva Nana' with twisted branches and a bun-shaped habit. Both turn somewhat bronze in winter.

Thuja occidentalis 'Rheingold'

An old yet always popular cultivar which was introduced in the early 1900s. Although classed as a dwarf it grows both upwards and outwards to cover a considerable area in time but can be trimmed to keep it in shape from its early

Thuja plicata 'Stoneham Gold'.

years. Foliage is both soft and feathery (juvenile) and open and coarse (adult) but even plants that start off with mostly juvenile foliage will eventually form adult foliage and the typical broadly pyramidal habit. Colour changes through the seasons from a rich copper in winter to yellow in early summer and old gold in late summer and autumn. Ideal in the heather garden against something like *Erica carnea* 'Springwood White' with which it makes a striking contrast.
H 90-120cm (3-4ft) × S 90-120cm (3-4ft).

Thuja occidentalis 'Smaragd'

Although I have recommended this strongly as a slower growing hedge for the smaller garden, it also makes a perfect accent plant when used as a specimen. Hardy as any conifer, it has the distinct advantage of holding its emerald green foliage colour through most of the winter, although I suppose the more extreme the climate the more likely it is to be tinged with bronze. Even so, most other green leaved forms of *T. occidentalis* go quite bronze and unattractive in winter. Except 'Smaragd', to make a neat and narrow pyramid some 2.5-3m (8-10ft) in ten years. Of slightly slower growth is *T.o.* 'Holmstrup', also raised in Denmark but an attractive specimen, broad at the base and narrowing to form an almost perfect cone.

Thuja occidentalis 'Sunkist'

This variety has proved to be one of the best dwarf golden conifers. It has a compact, broad pyramidal habit, bright golden yellow foliage in summer, toning down somewhat in winter to a more old gold colour.
H 1-1.2m (3-4ft) × S 90-120cm (3-4ft) at base.

'Sunkist' is only one of many somewhat similar, upright, golden foliaged forms or cultivars of the American arbor-vitae to be introduced in recent years. *T.o.* 'Europe Gold' is similar but more yellow than gold, rather faster growing, but both are superior to the incorrectly titled *T.o.* 'Lutea

Thuja occidentalis 'Holmstrup's Yellow'.

Nana' which makes a large round pyramid of more open habit reaching in ten years 2.5-3m (8-10ft). Perhaps best for winter colour is *T.o.* 'Holmstrup's Yellow', greeny yellow in summer but turning the brightest gold in mid winter, lasting well into spring. The foliage is inclined to scorch when the plant is small. Different again is *T.o.* 'Lutescens' with attractive, broad, flattened leaves tinged creamy white and the brighter *T.o.* 'Marrison Sulphur', broadly pyramidal, with dense sulphur yellow foliage, brighter in late winter than at any other time. Quite a choice, though if golds and yellows don't appeal there are many green varieties also available.

Thuja orientalis 'Aurea Nana'

Without doubt this is one of the most attractive and popular dwarf conifers of all and should find a sunny spot in every garden! It will never be an embarrassment with regard to excessive growth and, at the same time, it looks good even as a two to three year old plant. Oval in shape with densely arranged, vertical, almost laminated foliage sprays, rather bronzed in winter but turning a beautiful clear yellow in summer. H 60-75cm (24-30in).

Thuja plicata 'Stoneham Gold'

This is one of my favourites for winter colour. Slow growing, and in its younger years scarcely making an attractive form, its somewhat flattened foliage and branches are slow to make a bush. Even when young, however, it has bronze, green gold and yellow foliage all on the same plant—as bright in winter as in summer. Expect it to reach 60-90cm (24-36in) in ten years, though growth can be somewhat variable. So, too, can that of *T.p.* 'Rogersii' which, like 'Stoneham Gold' arose on the nursery of Rogers of Eastleigh in Hampshire, England, many years ago. 'Rogersii' slowly forms a rounded ball of congested bronze, green and golden foliage, although often more vigorous shoots develop. A distinct coppery shine is evident in winter. As with all golden-foliage conifers, best in a sunny position.

Tsuga, the Hemlocks

The hemlocks are a much underrated group of trees for ornamental use and although most of the species are too tall to be considered for the smaller or average garden, some, both dense in foliage and graceful in habit, should be considered where reasonable soil and drainage exists. There are now many dwarf and slow growing forms—most of these being selections of *Tsuga canadensis*, the eastern hemlock and introduced to gardeners in the United States, where the species is native. On this page only a few of these distinctive forms that add a form and texture all their own to the range of garden conifers can be mentioned. *Tsuga canadensis* and most of its varieties are lime tolerant—a useful advantage to many gardeners.

Tsuga canadensis 'Cole'

Also known as 'Cole's Prostrate', this makes a slow growing mat of foliage, gradually building up a central branching system, the older branches showing their age and character as the younger branches and shoots spread outwards and downwards. Perfect if placed to hang over a rock or wall on the rock garden.

H 10-15cm (4-6in) × S 75-100 cm (2ft 6in-3ft 6in).

More vigorous is *T.c.* 'Pendula', also known as 'Sargentii Pendula' or 'Sargent's Weeping Hemlock'. This plant would be completely prostrate unless trained upwards in its early years, making long slender stems with short green leaves. Most attractive when given some support from where it will cascade gracefully. Without trimming becomes a large specimen in time.

Tsuga canadensis 'Jeddeloh'

This represents two or three similar forms of dwarf hemlocks with a semi-prostrate habit. Pleasing as a small plant, as it grows it develops the attractive pendulous tips so characteristic of the species.

H. 30-45cm (12-15in) × S 60-75cm (24-30in).

Similar if rather broader in spread is *T.c.* 'Bennett' also known as 'Bennett's Minima'.

There are many more miniature varieties such as *T.c.* 'Rugg's Washington Dwarf', *T.c.* 'Minuta', ideal for the rock garden and for connoisseurs, and some with golden foliage, such as the much sought after *T.c.* 'Everitt's Golden', which makes a very slow growing, upright bush, and one or two selections with white tipped foliage. *T.c.* 'Dwarf White', certainly in time hardly dwarf, and *T.c.* 'Gentsch's White', denser in habit, are both worth keeping an eye open for.

Other conifers

This is, as you may have gathered, not a comprehensive work on conifers, and I have chosen the main and, to my mind, most important families from which to select. What have we omitted? No descriptions are given of individual plants among the following genera, but if you want to look further, use one of the books recommended in the last pages of this volume. All the genera of conifers are not represented below, just the main types generally available.

CEPHALOTAXUS – Close to the yews or Taxus, these are seldom offered or grown although some are quite interesting for garden use.

CRYPTOMERIA – There are many good garden conifers among the Japanese cedars though some of the dwarf forms are not hardy in a more severe climate than that of the British Isles. They come literally in all shapes and sizes and many colours.

CUPRESSUS – There are some excellent conifers represented among these cypresses though many are more suited to Mediterranean or Californian climates than more northerly locations. *Cupressus glabra* or *C. arizonica* are the hardiest of the species.

LARIX – The larches are generally fast growing deciduous trees but some very attractive dwarf forms can be found with some searching. These generally have to be propagated by grafting.

PSEUDOTSUGA – This family includes not only the well known Douglas fir, *P. menziesii*, but some attractive dwarfer forms for garden use. Almost looking like a cross between tsuga and taxus in foliage, they generally dislike chalk soils and can be temperamental, growing best in moist but well drained soils.

Tsuga canadensis 'Jeddeloh'.

Heathers– for year round effect

We have seen how to plant and grow heathers in the earlier pages of this book and have also seen ways of displaying conifers and heathers together to create an attractive year round garden. On these two pages are shown further examples of heather gardens or beds, with a distinct break between summer and winter. Even those that are not in their flowering season are attractive for their foliage and ground covering qualities. The Edens' garden shows what can be done in a similar sized garden or in a small border, but what principles should you adopt when designing your own heather beds and what other general uses are there?

There are no hard and fast rules but to my mind heathers are informal plants and so should be used informally. No straight lines, then, but use them in curved beds or groups within other plants. With a very small garden you may only have room for one of each, particularly if you become interested and want to have as large a collection as possible. There are in fact over 500 varieties in cultivation. However, when you do have sufficient space, try 3-15 plants of each. Bold groups *are* effective, particularly when used with contrasting flower and foliage colours. I like to intersperse winter and summer types, green summer foliage against golden foliage heathers and blue conifers. This can be achieved on

Calluna 'Sir John Charrington' in the winter snow.

Spring flowers make a pretty picture among the winter flowering heathers.

A study in foliage and flower contrasts.

Winter flowering heathers massed together in a Norfolk garden.

Winter flowering heathers.

A group of summer flowering heathers, *Erica cinerea* 'White Dale' in the foreground.

a small as well as large scale.

Because of the heathers' cheerful appearance in winter and early spring I think you should consider placing a bed or border within view of the house so that you can enjoy flowers while you are sitting indoors or washing the dishes. In the summer you may feel like going out into the garden more often and so summer flowers can be placed further away.

Your situation will, of course, determine what you can grow to some extent but remember that the southern aspect will catch the most light and colours will be considerably enhanced when you look from south to north, particularly in winter, when the sun doesn't get so far up above the horizon.

Conifers, heathers and some shrubs make a good year round mix, but try the more natural, dwarf spring flowering bulbs too. Dwarf perennials, alpines and dwarf shrubs provide additional form and colour, particularly in a small garden. In this situation don't be afraid to keep your heathers trimmed and go for those that are slower growing. There is always room for experimentation with plants and in learning you sometimes have to take a few chances.

A Calendar of flowering Heaths and Heathers

This is a guide to the approximate flowering times of a range of Heaths and Heathers which is by no means extensive. The flowering times will vary from season to season and according to location but it does indicate that you can have flowers during nearly every month of the year when a whole range of Heaths and Heathers is grown. There will also be seasonal interest from foliage colour.

Summer flowering heathers. *Calluna vulgaris* 'Peter Sparkes' in the foreground.

January
Erica carnea
  'Eileen Porter'
  'King George'
  'Myretoun Ruby'
  'Pink Spangles'
  'Praecox Rubra'
Erica x *darleyensis*
  'Arthur Johnson'
  'Darley Dale'
  'Furzey'
  'Silberschmelze'

February
Erica carnea
  'Aurea'
  'Carnea'
  'Eileen Porter'
  'Foxhollow'
  'King George'
  'Myretoun Ruby'
  'Pink Spangles'
  'Praecox Rubra'
  'Springwood Pink'
  'Springwood White'
  'Vivellii'
Erica erigena
  (mediterranea)
  'Alba'
Erica x *darleyensis*
  'Arthur Johnson'
  Darley Dale'

'Furzey'
'Jack H. Brummage'
'J. W. Porter'
'Silberschmelze'

March
Erica carnea
  'Aurea'
  'Carnea'
  'Eileen Porter'
  'Foxhollow'
  'King George'
  'Myretoun Ruby'
  'Pink Spangles'
  'Praecox Rubra'
  'Ruby Glow'
  'Springwood Pink'
  'Springwood White'
  'Vivellii'
Erica erigena
  (mediterranea)
  'Alba'
  'Brightness'
  'Superba'
  'W. T. Rackliff'
Erica x *darleyensis*
  'Arthur Johnson'
  'Darley Dale'
  'Furzey'
  'Jack H. Brummage'
  'J. W. Porter'
  'Silberschmelze'

April
Erica arborea
  'Alpina'
Erica australis
Erica carnea
  'Aurea'
  'Foxhollow'
  'King George'
  'Myretoun Ruby'
  'Pink Spangles'
  'Ruby Glow'
  'Springwood Pink'
  'Springwood White'
  'Vivellii'
Erica erigena
  (mediterranea)
  'Alba'
  'Brightness'
  'Irish Salmon'
  'Superba'
  'W. T. Rackliff'
Erica x *darleyensis*
  'Arthur Johnson'
  'Darley Dale'
  'Furzey'
  'J. W. Porter'
  'Silberschmelze'

May
Daboecia hybrid
  'William Buchanan'
Erica arborea

'Alpina'
Erica australis
Erica erigena
  (mediterranea)
  'Alba'
  'Brightness'
  'Superba'

June
Daboecia cantabrica
  'Alba'
  'Atropurpurea'
  'Donard Pink'
  'Hookstone Purple'
  'William Buchanan'
Erica cinera
  'Alba Minor'
  'Atrosanguinea
    Smith's Variety'
  'C. D. Eason'
  'Pink Ice'
  'Purple Beauty'
  'Velvet Night'
Erica tetralix
  'Alba Mollis'
  'Con Underwood'
  'Hookstone Pink'
  'Ken Underwood'
  'Pink Star'

July
Daboecia cantabrica

'Alpina'
Erica australis
Erica erigena
  (mediterranea)
  'Alba'
  'Brightness'
  'Superba'

'Alba'
'Atropurpurea'
'Donard Pink'
'Hookstone Purple'
'William Buchanan'
Erica ciliaris
  'Aurea'
  'Camla'
  'Corfe Castle'
  'David McClintock'
  'Stoborough'
Erica cinerea
  'Alba Minor'
  'Atrorubens'
  'Atrosanguinea
    Smith's Variety'
  'C. D. Eason'
  'C. G. Best'
  'Foxhollow
    Mahogany'
  'Golden Drop'
  'My Love'
  'Pink Ice'
  'Purple Beauty'
  'Velvet Night'
  'White Dale'
Erica tetralix
  'Alba Mollis'
  'Con Underwood'
  'Hookstone Pink'
  'Ken Underwood'
  'Pink Star'

August

Calluna vulgaris
  'Anne Marie'
  'Beoley Gold'
  'Blazeaway'
  'County Wicklow'
  'Darkness'
  'Foxii Nana'
  'Gold Haze'
  'H. E. Beale'
  'J. H. Hamilton'
  'Mrs Ronald Gray'
  'Multicolor'
  'Peter Sparkes'
  'Robert Chapman'
  'Silver Knight'
  'Silver Queen'
  'Sir John Charrington'
  'Sister Anne'
  'Sunset'
Daboecia cantabrica
  'Alba'
  'Atropurpurea'
  'Donald Pink'
  'Hookstone Purple'
  'William Buchanan'
Erica ciliaris
  'Aurea'
  'Camla'
  'Corfe Castle'
  'David McClintock'
  'Stoborough'
Erica cinerea
  'Alba Minor'
  'Atrorubens'
  'Atrosanguinea
    Smith's Variety'
  'C. D. Eason'
  'C. G. Best'
  'Foxhollow Mahogany'
  'Golden Drop'
  'My Love'
  'Pink Ice'
  'Purple Beauty'
  'Velvet Night'
  'White Dale'
Erica tetralix
  'Alba Mollis'
  'Con Underwood'
  'Hookstone Pink'
  'Ken Underwood'
  'Pink Star'
Erica vagans
  'Cream'
  'Lyonesse'
  Mrs D. F. Maxwell'
  'St Keverne'
  'Valerie Proudley'

September

Calluna vulgaris
  'Anne Marie'
  'Beoley Gold'
  'Blazeaway'
  'County Wicklow'
  'Darkness'
  'Foxii Nana'
  'Golden Carpet'
  'Gold Haze'
  'H. E. Beale'
  'J. H. Hamilton'
  'Mrs Ronald Gray'
  'Multicolor'
  'Peter Sparkes'
  'Robert Chapman'
  'Silver Knight'
  'Silver Queen'
  'Sir John Charrington'
  'Sister Anne'
  'Sunset'
Daboecia cantabrica
  'Alba'
  'Atropurpurea'
  'Donard Pink'
  'Hookstone Purple'
  'William Buchanan'
Erica ciliaris
  'Aurea'
  'Camla'
  'Corfe Castle'
  'David McClintock'
  'Stoborough'
Erica cinerea
  'Alba Minor'
  'Atrorubens'
  'Atrosanguinea
    Smith's Variety'
  'C. D. Eason'
  'C. G. Best'
  'Foxhollow Mahogany'
  'Golden Drop'
  'My Love'
  'Pink Ice'
  'Purple Beauty'
  'Velvet Night'
  'White Dale'
Erica tetralix
  'Alba Mollis'
  'Con Underwood'
  'Hookstone Pink'
  'Ken Underwood'
  'Pink Star'
Erica vagans
  'Cream'
  'Lyonesse'
  'Mrs D. F. Maxwell'
  'St Keverne'

October

Calluna vulgaris
  'H. E. Beale'
  'Peter Sparkes'
Daboecia cantabrica
  'Alba'
  'Atropurpurea'
  'Donard Pink'
  'Hookstone Purple'
  'William Buchanan'
Erica ciliaris
  'Aurea'
  'Camla'
  'Corfe Castle'
  'David McClintock'
  'Stoborough'
Erica cinerea
  'Alba Minor'
  'Atrorubens'
  'Purple Beauty'
Erica tetralix
  'Con Underwood'
  'Hookstone Pink'
  'Ken Underwood'
  'Pink Star'
Erica vagans
  'Lyonesse'
  'Mrs D. F. Maxwell'
  'St Keverne'
  'Valerie Proudley'

Winter flowering heathers. *Erica erigena* 'W. T. Rackliff' (white), and *Erica carnea* 'Myretoun Ruby'.

November

Erica x *darleyensis*
  'Arthur Johnson'
  'Darley Dale'

December

Erica carnea
  'Eileen Porter'
  'King George'
  'Praecox Rubra'
Erica x *darleyensis*
  'Arthur Johnson'
  'Darley Dale'
  'Furzey'
  'Silberschmelze'

This list is taken from 'An Adrian Bloom Gardening Guide' (to Heathers) published by Jarrold of Norwich.

Conifers for special purposes

By now you will probably have realised what a tremendous range of conifers there is and what a wide variety of uses they have. The lists on this page are intended to be a guide as to a possible selection for the purpose under which they are headed.

Conifers for groundcover.

For miniature gardens, troughs and sinks
Abies balsamea 'Hudsonia'
Chamaecyparis lawsoniana 'Gnome'
Chamaecyparis lawsoniana 'Ellwood's Pillar'
Chamaecyparis lawsoniana 'Minima Aurea'
Chamaecyparis obtusa 'Nana'
Chamaecyparis obtusa 'Nana Lutea'
Chamaecyparis pisifera 'Nana'
Chamaecyparis pisifera 'Nana Aureovariegata'
Cryptomeria japonica 'Vilmoriniana'
Juniperus communis 'Compressa'
Juniperus squamata 'Blue Star'
Picea abies 'Little Gem'
Picea glauca 'Echiniformis'
Picea glauca 'Alberta Globe'
Picea mariana 'Nana'
Pinus leucodermis 'Schmidtii'
Pinus mugo 'Humpy'
Pinus mugo 'Mops'
Thuja occidentalis 'Danica'
Thuja plicata 'Rogersii'

For winter colour
Abies lasiocarpa 'Compacta'
Chamaecyparis lawsoniana 'Minima Aurea'
Chamaecyparis lawsoniana 'Pygmaea Argentea'
Chamaecyparis lawsoniana 'Tamariscifolia'
Chamaecyparis obtusa 'Nana Lutea'
Chamaecyparis pisifera 'Filifera Aurea'
Chamaecyparis pisifera 'Gold Spangle'
Chamaecyparis pisifera 'Plumosa Aurea Nana'
Juniperus chinensis 'Aurea'
Juniperus chinensis 'Pyramidalis'
Juniperus x *media* 'Mint Julep'
Juniperus x *media* 'Old Gold'
Juniperus procumbens 'Nana'
Juniperus squamata 'Blue Carpet'
Juniperus squamata 'Blue Star'
Picea mariana 'Nana'
Picea omorika 'Nana'
Picea pungens 'Globosa'
Picea pungens 'Hoopsii'
Picea pungens 'Kosteri'
Picea pungens 'Hoto'
Pinus mugo 'Ophir'
Pinus parvifflora 'Glauca'
Pinus sylvestris 'Aurea'
Pinus sylvestris 'Moseri'
Taxus baccata 'Semperaurea'
Taxus baccata 'Standishii'
Thuja occidentalis 'Holmstrupp's Yellow'
Thuja occidentalis 'Lutea Nana'
Thuja occidentalis 'Rheingold'
Thuja occidentalis 'Sunkist'
Thuja plicata 'Rogersii'
Thuja plicata 'Stoneham Gold'

For large containers
(essential to keep well watered in summer)
Abies lasiocarpa 'Compacta'
Chamaecyparis lawsoniana 'Blue Nantais'
Chamaecyparis lawsoniana 'Ellwoodii'
Chamaecyparis lawsoniana 'Ellwood's Gold'
Chamaecyparis obtusa 'Nana Gracilis'
Chamaecyparis pisifera 'Boulevard'
Chamaecyparis pisifera 'Plumosa Aurea Nana'
Chamaecyparis pisifera 'Squarrosa Sulphurea'
Juniperus chinensis 'Kaizuka'
Juniperus chinensis 'Pyramidalis'
Juniperus chinensis 'Robusta Green'
Juniperus communis 'Hibernica'
Juniperus x *media* 'Mint Julep'
Juniperus x *media* 'Old Gold'
Juniperus scopulorum 'Skyrocket'
Juniperus virginiana 'Silver Spreader'
Picea glauca 'Albertiana Conica'
Picea omorika 'Nana'
Picea pungens 'Globosa'
Picea pungens 'Kosteri'
Pinus densiflora 'Umbraculifera'
Pinus nigra 'Compact Gem'
Pinus parviflora 'Glauca'
Pinus sylvestris 'Fastigiata'
Taxus baccata 'Fastigiata Aurea'
Thuja occidentalis 'Holmstrup'
Thuja occidentalis 'Rheingold'
Thuja occidentalis 'Sunkist'
Thuja orientalis 'Aurea Nana'
Thuja orientalis 'Conspicua'

For ground cover
Juniperus communis 'Repanda'
Juniperus horizontalis 'Blue Chip'
Juniperus horizontalis 'Hughes'
Juniperus horizontalis 'Glauca'
Juniperus horizontalis 'Plumosa Compacta'
Juniperus x *media* 'Mint Julep'
Juniperus x *media* 'Old Gold'
Juniperus x *media* 'Gold Coast'
Juniperus procumbens 'Nana'
Juniperus sabina 'Blue Danube'
Juniperus sabina 'Tamariscifolia'
Juniperus squamata 'Blue Carpet'
Juniperus virginiana 'Grey Owl'
Juniperus virginiana 'Silver Spreader'
Microbiota decussata
Taxus baccata 'Repandens'
Taxus baccata 'Summergold'

Soil testing

For any crop that you wish to grow, be it ornamental plants or vegetables, it is an advantage to know whether your soil is acid or alkaline (limy) and whether abundant in nutrients or short of them. From this position of knowledge you will be able to judge which plants you can grow best and what you need to apply to get the best results from them.

Nutrients are essential for all soils. That said, one can also add that the types of plants used in George and Angela Edens' garden are not demanding in their requirements and most soils, unless definitely starved or impoverished, would not require additional fertilizer. No fertilizers were used in the Edens' garden, for instance, at any stage.

Many plants require a soil which is not too acid and if too much acidity is the problem lime has to be added. For those gardeners wishing to grow many of the plants listed in this book, i.e. the summer flowering heathers—lime will definitely not be required to be added. Summer flowering heathers require an acid soil to thrive as do rhododendrons, azaleas and many other plants.

The acid test

There is a pH scale devised to measure whether a soil is acid or alkaline and by how much. This pH scale ranges from 1 to 14 with a neutral point of 7. Below 7 the soil becomes progressively more acid.

Most soils will lie between 4.5 and 8 and although there may be other kits available from retail outlets the most readily available is one made by Sudbury

A small sample of the garden soil is poured into the syringe.

The acid/alkaline (pH) test solution is added to the syringe.

The syringe is shaken and the liquid expressed into a specimen jar.

The colour of the liquid indicates the acidity. Check with the chart.

Technical Products. They offer a quite expensive do-it-yourself soil test kit to test for plant nutrients and pH. They also sell a much less expensive one for our purposes, the Lime Tester.

Testing procedure

Whether testing soil for nutrients or for pH level it is important to take samples from different areas in a large garden wherever there is an indication of a difference in soil quality. Keep these samples separate and labelled. Don't mix them together for testing. Soil samples should ideally be taken 5-8cm (2-3in) below the surface. Although soil test samples can be taken if the soil is not too wet the best time for adjusting the pH is in the autumn.

An auger, trowel or spoon is recommended to obtain the

samples, then allow them to dry naturally if very moist. Break up any lumps but avoid making a fine powder and remove any obvious solids such as small stones. Don't touch the samples with your fingers as contamination will give a false reading.

The operation is one in which some laboratory hygiene is required and it is important to follow the instructions carefully. The basic procedure for using the kit is illustrated and captioned on this page.

When you have your results you will be in a position to know what you should do, if anything, to your soil.

The above do-it-yourself test may be sufficient for most gardeners but many may prefer to get their soil professionally tested by sending away soil samples for complete analysis by experts. There are several companies who provide this service in Britain.

Altering the pH

For growing conifers and heathers a pH of 5.5 to 6.5 is ideal but both will grow successfully either side of these figures, though the summer flowering types must not go above the neutral pH of 7. So what to do if you want to grow acid loving heathers on an alkaline soil?

Alkaline soils to acid

Few people seem to be aware of how easy it actually is to reduce the pH, alkalinity or lime content of the soil. So many gardeners who want to grow acid loving plants such as rhododendrons and azaleas, autumn flowering gentians, summer flowering heathers, camellias and many other worthwhile shrubs give up or don't even consider growing these plants if their garden is on alkaline soil.

And yet, dare I say it, there is what appears to be an almost miraculous solution. This is flowers of sulphur, a product which has been commonly used as a fungicide, and which can be bought from chemists today. It seems to work well at reducing quite dramatically the pH of your soil. If you want a particular bed in your garden in which to grow summer flowering or foliage heathers and rhododendrons, here's what can be done:

1. Measure out the area in approximately the square yards or metres you want to cover.
2. Choosing a still day or evening, measure out some flowers of sulphur into a large pepperpot. (If you have no convenient container scatter the sulphur by hand, but wear gloves.) If the soil has a pH of 8—highly

alkaline—you should put the flowers of sulphur on at a rate of 95g per sq m (4oz per sq yd). The ground should have been dug thoroughly first and again after spreading so that the flowers of sulphur is mixed well with the soil. Then water thoroughly. It will not do any harm to plant soon afterwards. Within the year the pH should have reduced to a more reasonable 6.5 level (48g per sq m, 2oz per sq yd), should achieve half that reduction—if you have a neutral soil.)

We have proved the efficiency of this product ourselves at Bressingham. Though alkaline soils surrounding your bed could in time begin to raise the pH, more flowers of sulphur can maintain the required level. After three years of trials here, our treated area showed a pH level of 4.5 demonstrating the capability of flowers of sulphur to maintain the acidity of a soil which, naturally, has a pH of 6.5. It is worth remembering that it is also beneficial to add peat to the soil which will improve its structure. If you want to prove it for yourself, on a small scale, why not try a square metre or so first? Flowers of sulphur is normally only sold in small quantities.

Acid to alkaline

It is unlikely that you will wish to make your soil more alkaline than it is already but if the pH is down around 4 then an increase could be beneficial. Adding ground limestone at the rate of 190g per sq m (8oz per sq yd) should raise the pH by $\frac{3}{4}$ of a point. Soil low in organic matter i.e. humus will need about 25 per cent less. Soil high in organic matter could need as much as 100 per cent more but this extra should not be put on in one application.

Deterring cats and dogs

If your neighbourhood is overrun with cats and dogs, you may have to take steps to prevent them using your garden as a toilet and damaging your evergreen plants. There are at least two chemical deterrents available. Synchemicals offer one called Stay Off which, it is claimed, will deter animals and birds for up to eight weeks, depending on the weather. The chemical this and other brands contain is aluminium ammonium sulphate, which can also be obtained from a chemist. It becomes soluble after rain, obviously becoming less effective and requiring repeated applications at shorter intervals.

Another product is Pepper Dust. This is designed to keep dogs and cats sneezing rather than fouling and by all accounts is quite effective.

Pests and diseases

All plants have their enemies and problems and if they do occur then perhaps this page will have its uses in giving an indication as to what that problem might be and a possible means of prevention or control. This page should not change your mind that the type of plants and garden advocated are relatively trouble free—I hope I'm being honest in telling you what might occur to *some* plants, *some* seasons. Further information about pests and diseases can be obtained from *Garden Pests and Diseases of Flowers and Shrubs* by M. H. Dahl and T. B. Thygesen, published by Blandford Press, and *Collins Guide to Pests, Diseases and Disorders of Garden Plants* by S. Buczacki & K. Harris.

KEY	Plants referred to are mainly those described in this book.
ALL =	Conifers, heathers, dwarf shrubs and ground cover plants
C =	Conifers
GC =	Shrubs and groundcover plants
H =	Heathers

Pest	Plants affected	Symptom	Time of appearance	Treatment recommended Chemical	Product	Time of treatment
Adelgids	C	White cottonwool-like masses on the stems and new leaves. Leaf and stem galls or swellings.	Spring or autumn	Pirimicarb Pirimiphos-methyl	ICI Abol-G ICI Sybol 2	March and April also October to December. Choose a warm day when insect is most active.
Ants	ALL	Building of earth nests in heather causing the plant to die back.	Spring, summer, autumn	Gamma-HCH Pirimiphos-methyl	Murphy Ant Killer ICI Ant Killer	Use as directed when noticed.
Aphid (green and black)	ALL	Distortion and discolouring of leaves and black sticky deposits of honey dew.	Early spring until late autumn	Pirimicarb Permethrin Malathion Permethrin Pirimicarb Permethrin	ICI Abol-G Picket-G Murphy Malathion BIO Flydown ICI Rapid Murphy Tumblebug	Spray as a preventative in spring, otherwise when noticed.
Red spider mite	ALL	Browning and silvering of the foliage causing leaf drop in severe cases. Can be seen as minute orange red dot moving about under the leaf and stem.	Summer	Malathion Pirimiphos-methyl Dimethoate	Murphy Liquid Malathion ICI Sybol 2 Murphy Systemic Insecticide	Spray in May or early June as a preventive. Follow with second spray within two weeks, preferably on still, dry evening. Otherwise spray.

Disease

Pest	Plants affected	Symptom	Time of appearance	Treatment recommended Chemical	Product	Time of treatment
Conio-thyrium Pesta-lotiopsis	ALL C	Die-back of the leaves and in severe cases the stem as well. The dead leaves are often covered with minute black spots.	Spring until autumn	Benomyl Remove and burn dead tissue Carbendazim	PBI Benlate PBI Super Carb.	Spray when noticed. Chemicals mentioned can be mixed together at full rate for best results.
Mildew (powdery)	GC	White powdery deposits appear on the surface of the leaves. This is common in dry conditions.	Summer	Benomyl Bupirimate Thiophanate-methyl Dinocap	PBI Benlate ICI Nimrod-T. Murphy Systemic Fungicide PBI Toprose	Spray when noticed.
Mildew (downy)	GC	Whitish-grey, downy deposits appear in patches on the undersides of the leaves, particularly where water has been on the leaf surface.	Summer	Thiram Zineb Mancozeb	ICI General Garden Fungicide PBI PBI Dithane 945	Spray when noticed.
Phyto-phthora (root rot)	C H	Small dead section appears from the base of the stem first. Eventually the entire plant wilts and dies. Drought symptons are very similar and can often be confused with phytopthora.	Spring, summer and autumn	Dig up the affected plant with roots and burn it. Do not allow soil to drop elsewhere when moving. First try giving a soil drench with PBI Mancozeb, 1½kg in 250l of water. (10l of this solution on 1 sq. yd. repeated two times at fourteen day intervals). Replant with one heather. If this succumbs either a) remove surrounding soil completely and replace with fresh soil or compost or b) loosen soil and sterilize in situ with formaldehyde at rate of 5l per sq. yd. If plants nearby are likely to be contaminated by chemical remove soil and sterilize elsewhere. Replace when chemical has evaporated (two-three weeks). l = litre		Treat when noticed.
Rhizoc-tonia	H	Tip die back of stems and sharp bending of tip in right angle.	Spring, summer, autumn	Mancozeb Propiconazole	PBO Dithane 945 Murphy Tumbleblight	Spray when noticed.

Recommended books

Manual of Growing Conifers by Humprey J. Welch published by Theophrastus in New York, USA. A very authoritative work covering primarily dwarf and slow growing conifers. 490 pages and many black and white photographs. Mr. Welch has spent a great many years' research and, together with his first hand experience in gathering a collection and running a nursery, is well qualified in his subject.

An Illustrated Guide to Conifers by David Papworth, published by Salamander Books. A relatively small but useful guide with 150 illustrations, many taken at Bressingham. 160 pages.

Adrian Bloom's Guide to Garden Plants–Book 1 Heathers published by Jarrold & Sons, Norwich. Again a booklet which gives the beginner a basic introduction to the subject. 30 colour photographs of heathers and their uses.

Heathers in Colour by Brian and Valerie Proudley published by Blandford Press. 192 pages. 63 pages of useful introduction and cultural advice. 68 pages of colour plates, the remainder consists of descriptive lists of a great many cultivars.

The Gardeners' Book of Heathers by Geoffrey Yates published by Frederick Warne.

Conifers for your Garden by Adrian Bloom, published by Burall + Floraprint of Wisbech. Naturally I've put my own book first though not, I may add, because I think it necessarily the best. 148 pages, over 200 colour illustrations. 20 pages of introduction covering all aspects of conifers and their cultivation. Hardback.

Ornamental Conifers edited by Julie Grace, published in Britain by David and Charles, Newton Abbot, Devon. Mr Harrison, a New Zealander, travelled in many countries to take photographs for this superb book. 225 pages, 554 colour plates, full plant descriptions and cultural notes. Available in hardback.

Garden Conifers in Colour by Brian and Valerie Proudley published by Blandford Press, Poole, Dorset. A useful handbook with a 50 page introductory section, 118 colour plates and detailed descriptions of over 500 cultivars. Total 216 pages.

Adrian Bloom's Guide to Garden Plants – Book 2 Conifers published by Jarrold & Sons, Norwich. More a booklet than a book but relatively priced. 32 pages, 40 colour photographs giving a brief introduction to conifers.

A final note

Perhaps, if this book has aroused your interest in conifers and heathers you might like to read further on the subject in books which go into more depth than has been possible in this volume. Also included on this page and elsewhere in this book is information on products where manufacturers have been mentioned by name. I realise that by giving such information and even branded names I may be criticised since both can become dated very quickly but I felt the reader might still appreciate having this knowledge. Too often we are faced with advice to use 'a proprietary product' and are none the wiser as to what to look for.

However, I should also point out that although I have given names and products which, to the best of my knowledge, are among the best available, neither I nor the publisher can be held responsible for any problems or losses due to advice given.

Acknowledgements

I would like to thank Michael Warren for the excellent photography throughout this book, taken during the ten years of the garden's development.
I would also like to thank Fisons Ltd. for their help and particularly for their expert advice on the lawn.
Thanks are also due to the many individuals and companies who allowed use of their gardens, products or information.
Last, but not least, my thanks to George and Angela Edens for their forbearance and for giving me the opportunity to develop their garden.